BLACKBURN WITH DAR

Blackburn With Darwen

This book sh
Blackbu
be

DAR

red velvet & chocolate heartache

Harry eastwood believes that loving cake does not have to be a punishment, either for your health or for your waistline. As she has illustrated in both the British and US versions of *Cook Yourself Thin*, it's entirely possible to have your cake and eat it – if you know how . . .

Harry's passion for food is the driving force behind her writing. She sees food as a language, alive with ingredients. These characters behave in different ways, and have funny little habits of their own.

Harry is currently dividing her time between London and New York, working on various writing and television projects. She continues to love chocolate.

Light Chocolate Cake

red velvet & chocolate heartache

Harry eastwood

BANTAM PRESS

LONDON · TORONTO · SYDNEY · AUCKLAND · JOHANNESBURG

TRANSWORLD PUBLISHERS
61–63 Uxbridge Road, London W5 5SA
A Random House Group Company
www.rbooks.co.uk

First published in Great Britain in 2009 by Bantam Press, an imprint of Transworld Publishers

A CIP catalogue record for this book is available from the British Library.

ISBN 9780593062364

Addresses for Random House Group Ltd companies outside the UK can be found at:
www.randomhouse.co.uk
The Random House Group Ltd Reg. No. 954009

The Random House Group Limited supports The Forest Stewardship Council (FSC),
the leading international forest-certification organization. All our titles that are printed
on Greenpeace-approved FSC-certified paper carry the FSC logo. Our paper-procurement
policy can be found at www.rbooks.co.uk/environment

Photography: **Jean Cazals**
Additional Photography: **Tabitha Hawkins**
Design: **Lucy Gowans**
Art Direction: **Tabitha Hawkins and Harry Eastwood**
Food Styling: **Joss Herd, Annie Rigg and Harry Eastwood**
Props Styling: **Tabitha Hawkins**
Nutritional Information: **Judith Wills**

Typeset in Monotype Bembo and Serlio
Printed and bound in Great Britain by Butler Tanner & Dennis Ltd, Frome

2 4 6 8 10 9 7 5 3 1

Dear Max,

I wrote this book for you.

You're magic.

彤 x

CONTENTS

Have your cake . . .

This book is dedicated to lovers of cake.

Cake is not only
the most direct way
to put a smile on to a face,

it's also a mystery. I have always marvelled at the way that a disjointed pile of ingredients goes into a mixer and reappears from the oven, glorious and unified, looking and smelling nothing like it did before . . . The one who makes the cake is a magician, executing a delicate trick. The mystery of cake lies also in the panoply of tins sleeping in dark cupboards; the muffled whirring of machinery as the whisk churns and mixes together separate elements that look as if they could never get along; the licking of the spatula after it has wiped the bowl clean; and the sight of the rising cake through the oven door, solemn and silent.

I want to eat cake without guilt, disappointment, dissatisfaction or regret. And I don't want to take the hit for a cupcake that hides chemicals, or is devoid of any character,

life, or food benefits. Of all foods, cake is the most *fun* and, as such, shouldn't belong only to the élite (those with fast metabolisms who just 'don't diet', those who have no intolerances to wheat or dairy, or who have never had to take into account gall-bladder or cholesterol-related concerns).

There is a *lot* of average – even bad – cake out there. There are dry, slightly stale, tight cakes (with 'mean crumb' eyes that never smile); on the fluffy end of the scale are face-lifted sponges, with textures like margarine-coated air . . . quite innocent seeming, but indolent and puffed up with artifice.

> I didn't write this book because I'm obsessed with healthy food. I wrote it because I *adore* cake.

I didn't write this book because I'm obsessed with healthy food. I wrote it because I *adore* cake. The days of 'I really shouldn't' are over. I now consider good cake to be at the very heart of a healthy life, both for your body and soul.

The most important aspect of the cakes in this book is their gorgeous taste and texture, but I have also made a real effort to reduce the amount of fat and sugar (incidentally, I have found, without exception, that the cakes are actually improved by doing so).

Health *and* flavour are possible

There is no compromise between health and flavour – it's all possible at once, and in fact the two tend to go hand in hand. My aim is not just to reduce the fat and calorie content of cake, but also to add as much flavour, fluff or squidge as possible, so that the cakes themselves become the best that they can be.

It is commonly believed that so-called 'healthy food' must

be dull, without flavour, and even smug or patronizing. This is mostly unfounded – with the exception of 'diet food', which relies on bad or unnatural substitutions of ingredients. Hunting down cooking methods that honour ingredients rather than dissimulate them may require imagination and flair, but the answer to great-tasting, healthier cake is right under our noses.

By combining ground almonds (which are high in natural fat and provide the backdrop for Excellent Crumb) and finely grated vegetables (for fluff and moisture) *instead of butter*, you address the texture issue of cake head on, and improve it. It is an overlooked fact that butter, when it cools down, stiffens back to its original solid form, which can make the texture of traditional cakes chalky, even rigid. Also, there is a good dose of natural sugar in most root vegetables already, which is why these recipes are lower in added sugar than traditional ones.

Butter is king of the castle in the flavour department, and many delicious icings in this book are made from it. I'm all for butter – when you can *taste* it.

The dreaded 'd' word . . .

As someone who has tried every diet known to mankind (from the sublime to the ridiculous, the commonplace to the meticulous), I have no doubt that denial is dangerous. If you love cake, you simply must have it – but do it right. Make it ahead of time. Cut it into slices and freeze it. Anything to avoid falling on to that quadruple chocolate chip muffin at 4 o'clock that is loaded with useless and lethargic ingredients. Even when a given cake in this book is relatively naughty (compared to 'diet food' equivalents), you will glow as you hit two rather big birds with one (small) stone. Your cake craving will be absolutely quashed by how fantastic the cake is, and your body will receive a dose of goodness that dishes up some vitamins, and keeps you fuller and comforted for longer . . . What's more, a generous number of cakes are virtuously (even suspiciously) low in calories and fat, and will turn that 4 o'clock panic into Happy Hour.

For those of you interested in the calorie and saturated fat content of all these cakes, there is a chart on pages 182–4.

It's freezing in here . . .

Freezing the cakes is an absolute cinch. If you're super organized, you can even freeze the icing too, as long as you keep it in a separate container and don't ice the cake first. Simply let the cake or cupcake cool down until it's cold, before placing it flat in the freezer. It is always easier to put a cake or batch of cupcakes into a plastic bag once they are frozen solid. Freezing slices is a great way to make a lot of cake ahead of time and take it to work, to address those mid-morning Muffin Cravings.

A whole cake takes up to 4 hours to defrost at room temperature. Most cupcakes are ready within an hour and the baby cupcakes take only half an hour. A bowl or sealed plastic bag of icing will take no more than 2 hours but will definitely want a good beating before you use it.

Cake and Cinderella

Borrowing structure from vegetables to frame a cake is a bit like borrowing a pumpkin to make the carriage for Cinderella: it is simply an imaginative (but logical) swapping game.

Each and every vegetable used in these cakes has a different way of behaving, and brings something distinctive to the party. The combination of cake and vegetable is not an accidental union; in the context of that specific recipe, the ingredients belong together.

The 'water and wood theory'

I have a little vegetable theory that I like to call the 'water and wood theory', which helps to explain who the vegetables are, and what it is precisely that they bring to the cakes . . .

> Borrowing structure from vegetables is a bit like borrowing a pumpkin to make the carriage for Cinderella.

I often think of the 'wood' vegetables as being rather masculine. A 'wood' vegetable is able to weather change and withstand many different cooking conditions, without altering its fundamental structure. In other words, it's robust and will cook with stability even grated inside a cake; its 'woodiness' will remain a fundamental characteristic, whether raw or cooked.

Carrot and parsnip are the undisputed joint captains of the wood vegetables. Next (in order of 'woodiness') are beetroot, sweet potato and potato (the floury white varieties only), followed by butternut squash and pumpkin. The last two blend into a sub-category that might well be called 'silk', since this is the state they arrive at when cooked, but I'm splitting hairs.

A 'water' vegetable is characterized by its ability to

encourage and lift the other ingredients inside a cake. These vegetables don't provide the structure themselves, but will enhance, soften and support it. Please don't consider them less useful than the 'wood' vegetables. Just because they make less noise, doesn't mean that they don't have a voice.

'Water' vegetables are led by the diligent and extremely kind courgette. Turnip is also 'water' based, yet somehow retains a defiant 'wooden' collar, as if her back is gently resting against the wall for posture. Although swede is a bit of a rebel, (perfect in the damp and fragrant atmosphere of a drizzle cake), she is 'water' more than anything else.

As for aubergine, she's a one-off. Unique in her ability to empathize, she puts herself last, and gives away her lunch. She remains a devoted vegetable, with a noble spirit, a sensitive soul and a texture like velvet.

> Aubergine remains a devoted vegetable, with a noble spirit, a sensitive soul and a texture like velvet.

Cakes with characters

When I start a cake recipe, I have only a tentative sense of where I am going, or whom I might meet at the end of my journey. In the merry course of writing this book, I have come across some very wilful cakes: at times obnoxious or obedient, mischievous or naive, kind or boisterous, wise or impatient.

The behaviour of the vegetables inside cakes has always been a source of fascination, often of frustration, sometimes of huge amusement. Even now, after so many versions, I am moved by the way that aubergine rises and falls (like a breath) inside Heartache Chocolate Cake.

Red velvet graveyard

I was pretty depressed to realize that the fun didn't extend to pastry or biscuits. I created a Red Velvet Graveyard folder on my computer called 'Graveyard' for short. Over the course of six months, I tried to introduce these unreceptive blighters to the joys of vegetables . . . without success. After burying my disappointment and accepting defeat, I now see that it simply doesn't make sense to use vegetables in pastry and biscuits as it does in air-reliant structures such as sponges or scones. It still stings a little to think of the twenty or so recipes that I had dreamed up – Pear Tarte Tatin (with pumpkin pastry), or Spicy Gingerbread Men (made with parsnip biscuit).

Having said that, there are some rogue silver clouds in the sky that stem from these experiments. Parsnip Vanilla Fudge was an absolute pain in the neck, but is such wicked fun and so delicious that I refused to let it go . . . So I obstinately pursued it. As for Chocolate and Salted Caramel Squillionaire – well, I'm afraid that I just couldn't bear to cut out this inimitable character on account of its absolute scrumptiousness. The Squillionaire simply *refused* to be excluded (and, I'm afraid, always gets his own way)!

Although there is now no vegetable in the Squillionaire, he is just too good to lose, so let's all look the other way and pretend that we haven't noticed him.

> Although there is now no vegetable in the Squillionaire, he is just too good to lose.

Jams, jellies and juices

Jams, jellies and juices are best friends with cake, and therefore were automatically invited into this book. Like cake, they are good examples of vibrant natural products that are often ruined by being too sweet, or by other unnatural and unnecessary ingredients. The recipes for jams, jellies and juices in this book are nice and sharp, full of real colours and flavours – without any other rubbish. I believe they taste much better for letting the flavours of the fruit sing out, instead of being gagged by mountains of sugar.

Equipment

I consider a hand-held electric whisk, a set of scales, some measuring spoons, a large mixing bowl, a spatula, a roll of baking paper*, and the relevant tins to be the basics with which anyone can have fun making cakes. This book is designed to feed your enthusiasm for fantastic cake, not beat it out of you because you don't have any high-tech baking equipment at home.

Ingredients

I have tested all the recipes in the book using white rice flour as well as plain flour. This is partly because I like its lightness of texture, but also because I didn't want those with wheat intolerances to miss out on the fun. As a rule, I have found that most well-stocked supermarkets sell rice flour, and I would encourage anyone who hasn't yet baked with it to give it a go. Rice flour provides the cakes with a fluffiness and a lightness of touch that doesn't come with plain flour. However, if you choose to make your cakes with plain flour, simply substitute the quantity of rice flour in the recipes with

---

* There is a subtle but important difference between baking paper and parchment paper. The first is lightly lined with wax and will not require you to grease the surface that touches the cake (the other surface will need to be greased in order to glue it to the tin). Parchment will always require you to brush on a little oil. If you can find it, baking paper is a little less hassle than parchment.

the equivalent amount of plain flour.

I am equally fond of white spelt flour – especially in scones, because I find that it has a slightly harsh edge, which helps to shorten the scones. Doves Farm produces excellent white rice and spelt flours, and you can search for your nearest stockist at www.dovesfarm.co.uk. More information about specialist ingredients can be found on pages 180–1.

Goat's butter is another great ingredient. Goat's butter is less dense, so if using it instead of cow's milk butter to make icings from this book, you may need to increase the quantities of icing sugar a little in order to stiffen the mixture to the correct consistency.

> Rice flour provides the cakes with a fluffiness and lightness of touch that doesn't come with plain flour.

The salt issue: having been a bit of a self-confessed salt addict for years, I recently discovered that my body was not reacting happily to this affaire. As a result, I have been forced to cut down (out is too drastic) on this beloved poison. In most of the recipes, I advocate the use of $\frac{1}{4}$ tsp of salt, and sometimes, in the case of some scones, a $\frac{1}{2}$ tsp. It goes without saying that you should do whatever you like. By all means take it out completely; I will continue to include it (if only in tiny pinches) because I think that its presence adds something that would otherwise be missed (especially in chocolate-based recipes).

Although not strictly a seasonal book, there are recipes within these pages that do depend on seasonal ingredients (such as fruits, vegetables or flowers). Please don't be put off. Rather look forward to trying the recipe a little later in the year. If there is an option to replace a vegetable that may not be in season, the recipe will mention it. That said, I wholeheartedly approve of Maverick Behaviour, so feel free to swap courgettes for marrows, or carrots for sweet potatoes if you're feeling adventurous.

I urge you to bear the 'water and wood theory' in mind whilst playing, and always take into consideration hidden strong flavours. Beetroot, parsnip and turnip can be overpowering, and require tactful handling.

As a rule I have no problem using tinned or frozen fruit in cake recipes. The sponge is bound to react to the wetter ingredients with *slight* indignation. I therefore recommend that you do your level best to let them dry out on a plate covered in kitchen paper for at least half an hour before cooking. And don't beat yourself up when they sink to the bottom of the cake either – their shyness is to be expected and won't hurt the cake.

I draw the line at tinned or frozen fruit in jams. You're better off hunting for the best available jar in the shops, rather than fiddling with wet fruit that may not set properly.

> I wholeheartedly approve of Maverick Behaviour, so feel free to swap courgettes for marrows, or carrots for sweet potatoes if you're feeling adventurous.

Who's who . . .

Vegetables

Not only are these 'secret ingredients' low in calories and high in fibre, they are also bursting with essential nutrients that we should be consuming on a daily basis.

Aubergine

Low in calories and virtually fat-free, aubergines are rich in anti-oxidants and a phytonutrient that helps protect your brain cells from damage.

Beetroot

The juice of a beetroot might stain your dress, but it will never stain your health. The purply-red pigments that give beetroot its deep colour are rich in the compounds anthocyanin and saponin, which help to prevent any cholesterol in your system from damaging your arteries.

Butternut squash

Low in fat, butternut squash delivers an healthy dose of dietary fibre, making it an exceptionally heart-friendly choice. Its orange hue indicates its most noteworthy health perk: an abundance of powerhouse nutrients known as carotenoids to protect against heart disease.

Carrot

Carrots are nutritional heroes, goldmines of nutrients. They're jam-packed with carotene, which the body converts to vitamin A, essential for healthy vision. They really do help you see in the dark!

Courgette

Low in calories, courgettes also contain large amounts of folate, potassium and vitamin A.

Parsnip

What parsnip can offer your diet is threefold: its fibre content is great for digestion, its sweet taste is satisfying without being high in calories, and its potassium content helps to soothe feelings of anxiety, irritability and stress.

Potato

Potatoes are a useful source of vitamin C, vitamin B6 and potassium.

Pumpkin

Chock full of goodness, pumpkins are loaded with vitamins and minerals, and are especially high in carotenoids. These are really good at neutralizing free radicals – nasty molecules that can attack cell membranes and leave the cells vulnerable to damage.

Swede

There's much more to the humble swede than meets the eye – a good source of vitamin C, it's also high in anti-oxidants to help us live a long and healthy life.

Sweet potato

Much richer in nutrients than traditional potatoes, sweet potatoes are a good source of carbohydrates for diabetics and dieters. They're also a good source of vitamin A and provide vitamin E, which is so important to fertility that its original name is Tocopherol and roughly translates from Greek as 'to bring forth children'.

Turnip

Turnip is a stout little wonder containing sulphur compounds that are linked to cancer prevention.

Blackberries, Blueberries, Raspberries and Strawberries

If you've ever had the pleasure of picking fresh berries from a garden or in the woods, you already know how wonderful they are. These tiny, delicious fruits contain numerous health-promoting compounds known to protect against a plethora of health concerns, including ageing (wrinkles to you and me), heart disease and diabetes.

Lemons, Limes and Oranges

We all know that citrus fruits are high in vitamin C and that it's a powerful nutrient. What's more, oranges are a great source of soluble fibre, which helps control blood cholesterol levels.

Nuts and Seeds

All in all, nuts and seeds are the spark of life, a living food often described as perfect. Although they contain a large quantity of fat, much of it is in the form of essential fatty acids. Vitamins, minerals, amino acids and carbohydrates are just a part of their remarkable properties that can also boost your mood and increase your brain power.

Honey

One of the most natural forms of remedy, honey can act as a powerful antiseptic, and when eaten regularly may have anti-oxidant powers. It's also useful for diabetics as it has a less marked effect on raising blood sugar levels than sugar does.

Chocolate and Cocoa Powder

Generally, the more cocoa solids that chocolate contains, the more anti-oxidants and minerals it also contains. According to some research, cocoa powder has nearly twice the anti-oxidants of red wine, and up to three times the anti-oxidants found in green tea.

The case of the cases

The baking aisle of the supermarket can be a confusing place, apparently designed to bamboozle even the most ardent cake enthusiast. An exercise as straight forward as buying cupcake cases can be as slippery as black ice. I thought it useful therefore to include pictures of the three sizes of paper cases used in this book. This should help you with the business of choosing the right ones, without worrying about the names 'cupcake', 'muffin' and 'fairy cake' – all of which seem to be pointing at each other . . . With the correct paper cases, your cakes will rise beautifully and there will not be any mixture left over in the bowl.

The baking aisle of the supermarket can be a confusing place, apparently designed to bamboozle even the most ardent cake enthusiast.

P.S. Please don't try to make cupcakes either by pouring the mixture directly into the tray without the cases, or (which is just as silly!) by using cases without the support of the correct-sized muffin tray. I have tried both of these 'techniques' at some point in my cake career, and the results were an unmitigated disaster!

It's not you, it's the tin

The size of the tin in a cake recipe is more than an aesthetic concern, it's fundamental to the success of the recipe. The size of the tin determines the cooking time, and how much pressure or weight is put on a cake that is heaving itself upwards. A cake that sags in the middle is not quite cooked through (and in these instances the heart of the cake-maker may emulate the sunken and sad cake too).

A cupcake is not just a small cake, but a unit in itself.

baby cupcake
base diameter: 32mm
depth: 21mm

cupcake
base diameter: 50mm
depth: 38mm

muffin
base diameter: 50mm
depth: 50mm

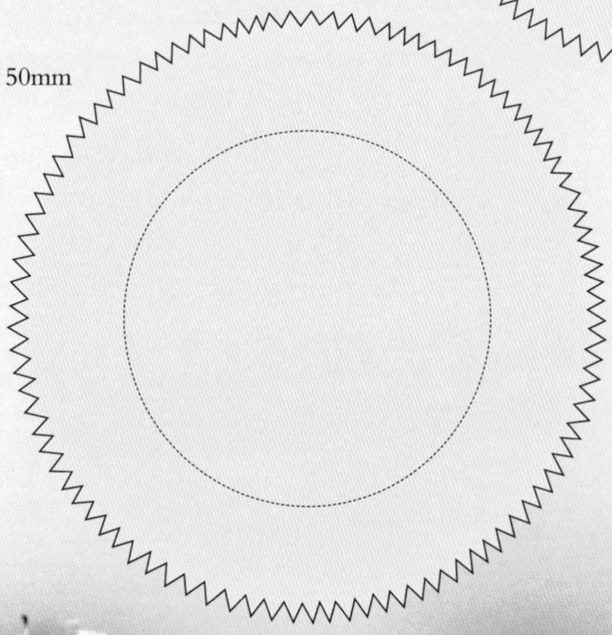

Similarly, a whole cake is *not* eight or twelve times a cupcake recipe – the two are separate entities. The cooking times and quality of the rise won't therefore convert consistently. It's important to the success of each recipe in this book that suggestions of tin and cupcake case sizes be followed as closely as possible.

Shortcuts and slip roads

I'm all for shortcuts if it makes life easier. You can trust me that if I advocate lining the base and sides of a tin in a slightly laborious fashion as I do in Autumn Apple and Cider Cake, and Beach and Blanket Fruit Cake, for example, it's because it's necessary and not just the silly old-school way. Incredible as it may sound, the success of a Great Cake sometimes relies on a factor as pedestrian as the correct lining of the tin. Incidentally, therein lies one of my secret favourite traits about cake: it is always its own wilful self. It is with a bob and a smile of respect that I have come to accept that some things in life just have to be done the long way.

Greasing the tins

The business of greasing the tins can be done by using either a bit of old butter paper and a small knob of butter, or a pastry brush with a little light oil (you're better sticking to vegetable oil as olive won't taste nice). I prefer to use a pastry brush or a clean paintbrush from the hardware shop, as they deliver the best results. Avoid new-fangled brushes with plastic 'hair', as they just slather on too much oil and make the cake greasy.

Getting your ducks in a row

If you are tidy-minded, you may be tempted to line up your ducks before you start making a cake. This will remind you of just how easy it can be to make a beautiful cake. My only word of caution is: *please* don't grate the vegetable until you are about to add it to the mixture. Its texture will not improve by sitting there. Most vegetables tend to lose their feathers once they are grated. They just get cold, wet and a bit grumpy.

Remember that the texture of each cake is entirely linked to the size of the vegetable shred. All the vegetables in this book should be grated very finely (unless otherwise specified), in order to keep them light and full of air. This also applies to zests, since these need to be feather-like or they will not distribute the flavour evenly. I have used a box grater on the smallest shred and found it all right, but I advise you to invest in a separate fine grater. A new one will take half the time and muscle power to grate than an old box one. I recommend a Cuisipro grater for this exercise (see page 179 for stockists). In order to provide the cake with the best possible crumb, the grating should be done by hand rather than in a food processor.

Most traditional cake recipes call for a skewer to determine whether the cake is ready or not. You can use this method if you are familiar with it, but beware: in the case of vegetable cakes, the skewer will often come out a little messy, *even* when the cake is cooked through. This is because of the moisture in the vegetables, and is perfectly normal. If a particular colour or look is an indicator of the readiness of a cake, the recipe will always tell you so. I recommend following the stated cooking times and simply looking through the glass of the oven door (or taking a *very* quick and furtive peek inside if you don't have a glass oven door) to observe whether the cake has risen evenly. If you see a slight dip in the middle, leave the cake in for an additional 5 minutes, then check it again. Repeat every 5–7 minutes until you are confident that the cake is cooked. This checking method will not *correct* a dip, but does ensure as little damage as possible.

One final word of caution: all butter icings must go on to *cold* cakes, as opposed to *cool* ones. There is a treacherous amount of heat left inside a cool cake and this will turn the icing into a landslide, rather than the stiff and elegant mountain-side it should be. The landslide is not a good look . . .

Finally . . .

The only thing left to say to you is: enjoy the cakes. Have fun! Don't be afraid of them and giving them a go. You're bound to find the right one for you; the one that understands you or makes you feel uplifted. The one that you will make over and over again. The one that's yours.

These cakes can't wait to be made and talked about. After all, everyone likes to have nice things said about them . . .

HAPPY COOKING!

BIRTHDAY CAKE

Birthday Cake

Birthday Cake is so naughty, it should be illegal. She's everything that you're not allowed: ice cream for breakfast, jumping up and down on the bed, and hundreds and thousands sandwiches . . . She has a brave streak, and delights in living another year.

SERVES 12

4 medium free-range eggs
200g caster sugar
400g topped, tailed,
     peeled and finely
     grated courgette
220g white rice flour
140g ground almonds
3 tsp baking powder
¼ tsp salt
finely grated zest of
     3 unwaxed lemons

FOR THE ICING
50g unsalted butter,
     softened
2 tbsp freshly squeezed
     lemon juice
200g icing sugar, sieved

FOR THE FILLING
200g Sharpie Strawberry
     Jam (see page 7)
     or good-quality
     shop-bought
     strawberry jam

FOR THE TOP
hundreds and thousands,
     silver balls, dolly
     mixtures

YOU WILL NEED
three 18cm-diameter
     x 5cm-deep loose-
     bottomed tins

1 Preheat the oven to 180°C/350°F/gas mark 4. Using a pastry brush, lightly oil the base and sides of the tins. Line the bottoms with baking parchment and brush again with a little more oil.

2 Start by whisking together the eggs and sugar for 5 minutes until pale and full of air. Next, add the grated courgette and whisk until combined. Finally, add the flour, ground almonds, baking powder, salt and lemon zest. Beat this mixture until it feels unified.

3 Divide the mixture evenly between the three tins and place in the middle of the oven. Bake for **30 minutes**.

4 Take the cakes out of the oven, unmould them, peel off the parchment and let them cool on a wire rack for at least 30 minutes before icing.

5 To make the butter icing, whisk the butter until you reach a smooth paste. Add a little of the lemon juice and a little icing sugar before beating again. Continue this process, alternating between the icing sugar and lemon juice until both are all used up.

6 To assemble the cake, simply sandwich the layers of cake with jam and spread the icing over the top, before scattering it with hundreds and thousands, silver balls and sweets.

TRUST ME TIPS

• Don't let the grated courgette sit for too long, or it will start to become limp and liquid. It's best to work quickly once the vegetable is grated.

STRAWBERRIES AND CREAM CUPCAKES

THERE ARE TWO WEEKS of the calendar that are sacred, and summed up in one single word: Wimbledon. These cupcakes are rather like the ball boys and girls, who fizz about the court: discreet, tidy and perfectly on time.

MAKES 12

2 medium free-range
    eggs
160g caster sugar
200g topped, tailed,
    peeled and finely
    grated **courgette**
1 tsp vanilla extract
100g white rice flour
100g ground almonds
2 tsp baking powder
¼ tsp salt

FOR THE FILLING

½ pot Sharpie Strawberry
    Jam (see page 7)
    or good-quality
    shop-bought
    strawberry jam

FOR THE ICING

50g unsalted butter,
    softened
150g icing sugar, sieved
50g mascarpone

FOR THE TOP

12 fresh strawberries

YOU WILL NEED

a 12-hole muffin tray
12 cupcake cases (see
    page xxvii for
    exact size)

1 Preheat the oven to 180°C/350°C/gas mark 4 and line the muffin tray with the paper cases.

2 Whisk up the eggs and sugar in a large mixing bowl until they are pale and fluffy (this takes 4 minutes of solid whisking).

3 Whisk the grated courgette and the vanilla extract into the egg mixture until well incorporated. Finally, whisk in the flour, ground almonds, baking powder and salt until everything is completely combined.

4 Using a large spoon, ladle a couple of generous spoonfuls of the mixture into the bottom of each paper case. Add a teaspoon of jam, then cover that with a small spoonful of mixture, in order to seal in the jam. The ratio should be roughly two thirds cake mixture at the bottom of the cupcake, then the jam, then one third cake mixture to finish. If you only leave a little bit of cake mixture for the top, you end up with the jam bleeding and splitting out of the top of the cupcake.

5 Place in the oven for **20 minutes** until risen and blonde on top. Once the cupcakes are cooked, cool them in the tin for 10 minutes. After this, cool them down completely in the fridge for a further 20 minutes, as they need to be cold before icing. Whilst the cupcakes are cooling, make the icing.

6 Beat the butter with 50g of the icing sugar by hand, in a large mixing bowl. It is best to use the back of a wooden spoon here. Grind the icing sugar into the butter until you reach a paste. At first it will look as if it won't mesh, but it does blend in the end.

7 Using the same technique, mix in the next 50g of sugar and the mascarpone until you have a paste. Finally, add the last 50g of sugar, which should combine easily and correct any possible curdling effect from the previous stage. Refrigerate until the cakes have cooled completely.

CONTINUED OVERLEAF

8 Ice each cold cake with the help of a knife, using a small tablespoonful of the icing each time. Top with a strawberry and return to the fridge to set the icing. If serving much later on, keep the cakes in an airtight container in the fridge for up to two days, taking them out half an hour before serving.

TRUST ME TIPS

- It is important to follow the steps for the icing in this order, adding the sugar gradually and not all at once. This method produces fluffy and light icing that is together and happy, rather than over-sweet and split. Don't be tempted to beat the icing with a whisk here, as it will liquidize the mascarpone and alter the togetherness of the texture.

- Feel free to change the flavour of this cupcake by replacing the jam in the middle and the fruit on top. I have tried this with apricots (when they are really ripe) and apricot jam, as well as with blackberry jam and blackberries. Raspberries work really well too.

SHARPIE STRAWBERRY JAM

I KNOW SOMEONE who *is* this jam. She sometimes lacks tact and gets the pips stuck between her teeth, but when she's happy her eyes glitter like dark beads on her pretty face. At the moment, she's lying on the floor, glued to the tennis on the box and eating jam out of the jar with a spoon.

MAKES 1 LITRE

1.2kg **strawberries** (starting weight), hulled and cut into quarters

600g jam sugar (with added pectin; also called preserving sugar)

200ml freshly squeezed lemon juice (roughly 3 lemons)

YOU WILL NEED

four or five jam jars with lids

a timer

1 Preheat the oven to 100°C/200°F/gas mark ¼ and place the jam jars, with their lids separately, inside. This will sterilize them and warm them so that the glass doesn't crack under the pressure of the hot jam. Remove them from the oven 10 minutes before the jam is finished.

2 Rinse the hulled and quartered strawberries briefly under the tap and sit them in a colander to drain. Combine all the ingredients in a large saucepan. Start the heat on the lowest setting until you have completely dissolved the sugar. This stage will take 15 minutes and should not be rushed or the sugar will crystallize.

3 Bring to the boil. Set your timer when you reach the first signs of a full boil, where the bubbles are constant and fairly big, for 10 minutes, and leave the pan uncovered. With the help of a large spoon and a small plate, remove any pale-coloured scum that appears on the surface. Repeat this process throughout the cooking time. It's also really important to regularly scrape the bottom and in the corners of the pan to prevent any sticking and burning.

4 Once the 10 minutes are up, ladle the hot jam carefully into the prepared jam jars and seal the lids on. Leave to cool and set for 2 hours before tasting.

TRUST ME TIPS

• I have chosen to quarter the strawberries because I prefer a jam with no big lumps of fruit. In this recipe the jam is relatively uniform. If you would rather have a chunkier jam, follow the recipe in exactly the same way but don't bother quartering the strawberries.

• The saucepan needs to be really quite big, since jam has a habit of creeping up the sides of the pan. It is also important to use a big pan so that the fruit is evenly covered by its own juice.

RASPBERRY CORDIAL

IMPETUOUS, WITH A FACE full of freckles and a flame of red hair, this cordial looks at the world with eyes wide with anticipation. She swings between rapture and despair, and lives for blossom, poetry, and tea served with cake and cordial.

MAKES 850ML

600g fresh
    raspberries
175ml freshly squeezed
    lemon juice
    (roughly 2 lemons)
450g caster sugar
400ml water

YOU WILL NEED

one or more glass
    bottle(s) with lid(s)
a timer

1 Start by sterilizing the bottle(s) in which you plan to keep the cordial. Preheat the oven to 100°C/200°F/gas mark ¼. Place the bottle in the oven, with its lid by its side, when you start making the recipe. Remove from the oven just before using. Don't worry if the cordial sizzles a tiny bit when you're pouring it into the bottle – that's quite normal.

2 Place the raspberries in a large saucepan and strain the lemon juice over them through a sieve. Bring this mixture to the boil and simmer gently for 5–7 minutes until all the fruit has lost its shape, and all that is left in the saucepan is red juice and a lot of pips.

3 Pass this through a fine-mesh sieve, one heaped tablespoon at a time. By all means press down hard on it with the back of a spoon. I find that it helps to scoop it up and spread it over the wire a few times, just as an old-fashioned washerwoman might handle a stubborn stain. With a clean spoon, scoop up the juice and pulp that has gathered underneath the sieve and let that fall into the red mixture.

4 When you're quite sure that you've squeezed every ounce of juice from the seeds, discard them and repeat the process until you've used up all the mixture. You'll obtain somewhere in the region of 450ml of bright red juice. Set this aside whilst you make the sugar syrup.

5 Start by dissolving the sugar with the water in a saucepan on a low heat until all the sugar crystals have disappeared completely. Bring to the boil and boil hard for 5 minutes exactly (start timing only when you have the mixture boiling hard). The bubbles will creep up the sides of the pan, so don't go anywhere, but rather keep a sharp eye on what's going on. My advice is not to leave the pan at all during the sugar-syrup stage of this recipe as it's just too dangerous. The sugar syrup is dying to be given an excuse to crystallize and spoil the fun.

6 The clear sugar bubbles will start small, but as the minutes race by they'll get bigger and bolder. They'll look the size of transparent walnuts just before the syrup is ready, so watch out for the change. During the sugar-syrup-making stage, it is important to let the

bubbles do their own thing. Don't be tempted to stir or fiddle with the pan in any way, as the bubbles hate this and will punish your curiosity by crystallizing. The cleaning of a pan with crystallized sugar in it is just horrid.

7 It is possible, and rather necessary, however, to test the sugar syrup to check what stage it is at. To do this, simply hold a metal spoon in your hand for 30 seconds to warm it up, then dip the back of it quickly into the mixture. Bring it out and wait for 10 seconds to see if the liquid runs off it. You will have reached the correct sugar-syrup stage when the mixture gently coats the back of the spoon. As soon as you get to this point, remove the pan from the heat and let it stand for 10 minutes. Not only will this prevent the sugar syrup from galloping ahead of itself and going too far, it will cool and thicken it *just enough* to syrupify the raspberries and bring the cordial together.

8 Once the syrup (which will measure around 480ml) has cooled for the correct amount of time, add the strained raspberry juice and mix well. Decant into a sterilized bottle and put on the lid. Once opened, store in the fridge. Dilute one part cordial to four parts water.

TRUST ME TIPS

• This raspberry cordial is lovely mixed with white wine or champagne for a different, home-made sort of kir/kir royal.

Lemon Drops, Orange Blossoms, Ginger Millies

LEMON DROPS

BARELY A MOUTHFUL of this provocative blonde bombshell is enough to deliver a citrus hit that will endure in your mind for years.

MAKES 24

1 medium free-range egg
50g caster sugar
100g topped, tailed,
    peeled and finely
    grated **courgette**
25g white rice flour
50g ground almonds
1 tsp baking powder
small pinch of salt
finely grated zest of 2
    unwaxed lemons
1 tsp lemon extract
a little dash of yellow
    food colouring paste
    (see page 180
    for stockists)

FOR THE ICING
150g icing sugar, sieved
2 tbsp freshly squeezed
    lemon juice
a tiny amount of yellow
    food colouring paste

FOR THE TOP
a little lemon zest

YOU WILL NEED
two 12-hole baby
    muffin trays
24 baby cupcake cases
    (see page xxvii for
    exact size)

1 Preheat the oven to 160°C/325°F/gas mark 3 and line your muffin trays with the paper cases.

2 Whisk together the egg and sugar in a large mixing bowl for 3 minutes, until fluffy and pale. Add the grated courgette and beat again until fully incorporated.

3 Add the flour, ground almonds, baking powder and salt, as well as the grated lemon zest, the lemon extract and the food colouring. Give one final whisk for a minute or so, to make sure that all the ingredients are mixed up together.

4 With the help of two teaspoons (one to scoop up the mixture, the second to scrape it into the case neatly), carefully plop a small dollop of the mixture into each case, making sure to leave a little space (say half a centimetre) at the top. Bake for **15 minutes**, while you prepare the icing.

5 To make the icing, simply combine the sugar and lemon juice with a fork or sauce whisk until smooth. Run a little colouring paste through it (with the end of a toothpick) until you arrive at a satisfactorily provocative shade of yellow. If using the icing at a much later stage, place a sheet of cling film directly on to the surface to prevent it from forming a skin.

6 Remove the cakes from the oven and cool for 15 minutes on a wire rack.

7 Once cooled, ice the Lemon Drops individually with a teaspoon. The sharp flavour of the icing is just perfect for the cake and should make up a layer roughly 2mm thick − more of a hat than a comb, if you catch my drift.

8 Finally top with a little zest for added vibrancy and violins. Keep in an airtight container for up to 2 days.

CONTINUED OVERLEAF

• The lemon zest needs to be grated into very small shreds, otherwise the flavour doesn't get a chance to spread out evenly – the smaller the better.

• The yellow food colouring is a little something that I love to put into the icing of these Lemon Drops, especially if I am making a couple of different flavours of cake. They look so great on a plate with Orange Blossoms and Ginger Millies (see pages 13 and 15).

ORANGE BLOSSOMS

THESE LITTLE CUPCAKES are light, bright and pretty. They're also a little fickle, and not without ambition. Don't be surprised if they compliment you on your hair, the week before your birthday party invitations are being handed out . . .

MAKES 24

1 medium free-range egg
50g caster sugar
100g peeled and finely
  grated **butternut**
  squash
finely grated zest of
  1 orange
1 tsp orange blossom
  water
25g white rice flour
50g ground almonds
1 tsp baking powder
small pinch of salt
  (optional)

FOR THE ICING
125g icing sugar, sieved
1 tbsp fresh orange juice
1 tsp orange blossom water
1 tsp freshly squeezed
  lemon juice
a little orange food
  colouring paste
  (see page 180
  for stockists)

FOR THE TOP
tiny white flowers or
  blossoms

YOU WILL NEED
two 12-hole baby
  muffin trays
24 baby cupcake cases
  (see page xxvii for
  exact size)

1 Preheat the oven to 160°C/325°F/gas mark 3 and line your muffin trays with the paper cases.

2 Whisk together the egg and sugar in a large mixing bowl, until fluffy and pale – this should take no more than a couple of minutes. Add the grated butternut squash and orange zest, along with the orange blossom water, and beat again until fully incorporated.

3 Finally, add the flour, ground almonds, baking powder and salt (if using) to the mixture. Give one final whisk for a minute or so, to combine all the ingredients.

4 With the help of two teaspoons (one to scoop up the mixture, the second to scrape it into the case neatly), carefully plop a small dollop of the mixture into each case, making sure to leave a little space (say half a centimetre) at the top.

5 Holding the muffin tray with both hands, give it four or five bangs on the kitchen surface to level the tops. Be assertive, but not so keen that you jump them out of their little slots. Bake for **15 minutes**, whilst you prepare the icing.

6 To make the icing, simply combine the icing sugar, orange juice, orange blossom water and lemon juice with a fork or sauce whisk until smooth. Run a tiny bit of orange colouring (with the tip of a toothpick) through the mixture. Be aware that a tiny amount of colouring goes really far . . . If using at a much later stage, place a sheet of cling film directly on to the surface of the icing to prevent it from forming a skin.

7 Remove the cakes from the oven and cool for 15 minutes on a wire rack.

8 Ice the Blossoms individually with a teaspoon. One teaspoonful per baby cake should be just the right amount. Finally, add your little flowers or blossom sprigs before serving.

• Orange blossom water isn't my favourite flavour in the sweetshop, so I have gone more for a hint than a hit of the stuff here. In small doses, it reminds me faintly of apricot and spring breezes; in large doses, of soap and my grandmother's powder compact! As long as you stick to the correct amount of liquid in relation to the icing sugar, feel free to fiddle with the flavour.

GINGER MILLIES

THESE LITTLE CUPCAKES always keep their promises but also have a keen eye for a joke . . . They delight in whoopee cushions, stinks bombs, and watching you pour salt into your morning cup of tea.

MAKES 24

1 medium free-range
    egg
50g caster sugar
100g peeled and finely
    grated **butternut
    squash**
finely grated zest of ½
    unwaxed lemon
25g white rice flour
50g ground almonds
1 tsp baking powder
2 tsp ground ginger
small pinch of salt
    (optional)
a little pink food
    colouring paste
    (see page 180
    for stockists)

FOR THE ICING

125g icing sugar, sieved
2 tsp fresh lemon juice
1 tbsp water
pink food colouring paste

FOR THE TOP

a pinch of hundreds
    and thousands

YOU WILL NEED

two 12-hole baby
    muffin trays
24 baby cupcake cases
    (see page xxvii for
    exact size)

1 Preheat the oven to 160°C/325°F/gas mark 3 and line your muffin tray with the paper cases.

2 Whisk together the egg and sugar in a large mixing bowl until fluffy and pale – this should take no more than a couple of minutes. Add the grated butternut squash and lemon zest, and beat again until fully incorporated.

3 Add the flour, ground almonds, baking powder, ground ginger and salt (if using) to the mixture. Give one final whisk for a minute or so, to make sure that all the ingredients in the bowl are combined. Add a tiny dash of colouring paste to the mixture to turn it pale pink.

4 With the help of two teaspoons (one to scoop up the mixture, the second to scrape it into the case neatly), carefully plop a small dollop of the mixture into each case, making sure to leave a little space (about half a centimetre) at the top. Bake for **15 minutes**, whilst you prepare the icing.

5 Once all the cases are filled with ginger-coloured mixture, hold the tray with both hands and bang it frankly on the surface 4 or 5 times. Frankly means with decision and a little force, enough to shake the mixture flat, but not enough to make the little cupcakes jump out of their skin and make a mess.

6 To make the icing, simply combine the icing sugar, lemon juice and water with a fork or sauce whisk until smooth. Run a little colouring paste through it (with the tip of a toothpick) until you arrive at a shade that looks like pink cheeks. Beware: a tiny amount of colour goes a very long way . . . If you are not using the icing until much later, place a sheet of cling film directly on to the surface to prevent it from forming a skin.

7 Remove the cakes from the oven and cool them for 15 minutes on a wire rack.

8 Ice the Millies individually with a teaspoon. Finally, add your pinch of hundreds and thousands before serving.

CONTINUED OVERLEAF

• You could also use red food colouring, which would colour the icing pink too, if you promise to use only a microscopic amount.

• The mixture might appear quite stiff and not very spongy, but it becomes lovely and fluffy when the butternut squash cooks and all the ingredients melt together into magical sponge.

• If you like your Millies to be quite fiery, choose organic ground ginger, which is significantly stronger.

CHOCOLATE CHOCOLATE CHIP CUPCAKES For Becky

THIS BRAVE LITTLE CUPCAKE says: 'I'm going to have it, and I'd like it *all*, please.' She has an air of determined defiance, and is willing to wait for as long as it takes to prove a point worth making.

MAKES 12

3 medium free-range
    eggs
180g Demerara sugar
250g topped, tailed,
    peeled and finely
    grated carrot
2 tbsp strong coffee (or
    boiling water if you
    don't like coffee)
120g white rice flour
50g ground almonds
40g good-quality cocoa
    powder
2 tsp baking powder
¼ tsp salt
100g chocolate chips
    (any colour you like)

FOR THE TOP
1 quantity Naughty
    Chocolate Icing
    (see page 101)
a few shavings of
    chocolate for
    decoration

YOU WILL NEED
a 12-hole muffin tray
12 paper cases (see page
    xxvii for exact size)

1 Preheat the oven to 180°C/350°F/gas mark 4 and line the muffin tray with paper cases.

2 In a large mixing bowl, whisk together the eggs and sugar for a full 5 minutes, until the mixture is quadrupled in volume and extremely fluffy.

3 Whisk in the carrot and coffee. When they are fully incorporated, beat in the flour, ground almonds, cocoa powder, baking powder and salt with the help of an electric whisk until they are well combined. Fold in the chocolate chips with a metal spoon until they are scattered hither and thither.

4 Spoon the mixture into the paper cases so that it comes four fifths of the way up the sides.

5 Cook in the middle of the oven for **25 minutes**. Cool in the tin for 10 minutes, then at room temperature for another half-hour until cold. If you are in a hurry to eat them, put them into the fridge at this stage. The important thing to remember is that they must be cold when you ice them.

6 Whilst the cupcakes are cooking, make the Naughty Chocolate Icing. Ice when the cupcakes are cold, with the help of a small knife or spatula.

TRUST ME TIPS

• If your carrots are very fresh, there is no need to peel them – simply give them a good wash, then top and tail them. When carrots get a bit older, their skin becomes a little bitter.

• Feel free to up the amount of chocolate chips by 50g (any more and the mixture will drag down too much) to make these cakes even more irresistible. I also sometimes do this if I don't have time to ice them to make them more chocolatey and delicious.

ORANGE SQUASH CUPCAKES

THESE CUPCAKES BELONG to July picnics with squashed sandwiches, cotton dresses, Scotch eggs and cartons of juice.

MAKES 12

2 medium free-range
    eggs
160g caster sugar
200g peeled and finely
    grated butternut
    squash
finely grated zest and
    juice of 1 orange
    (juicing varieties,
    such as Seville,
    are best)
100g white rice flour
100g ground almonds
2 tsp baking powder
¼ tsp salt

FOR THE ICING

75g unsalted butter,
    cold and cubed
200g icing sugar, sieved
finely grated zest of
    1 orange
1 tbsp freshly squeezed
    orange juice

FOR THE TOP

a little grated orange
    zest

YOU WILL NEED

a 12-hole muffin tray
12 paper cases (see page
    xxvii for exact size)

1 Preheat the oven to 180°C/350°F/gas mark 4 and line the muffin tray with paper cases.

2 Whisk the eggs and sugar in a large mixing bowl for 5 minutes, until pale and quadrupled in volume. Add the grated butternut squash and orange zest, and whisk again. Mix in the flour, ground almonds, baking powder and salt, along with the orange juice, until they are well introduced.

3 Spoon the mixture into the cupcake cases, aiming for it to come four fifths of the way up each case. Place in the oven for **20 minutes** until risen and cooked. Don't be alarmed that they are flat on the top rather than dome shaped. Cool in the tin for 15 minutes, before refrigerating until cold enough to ice.

4 Whilst the cupcakes are cooling, make the icing. Whisk the butter in a large mixing bowl with an electric whisk until pale and fluffy before adding 100g of the icing sugar. Whisk again to incorporate the sugar. Add the orange zest and juice, as well as the remaining sugar. Beat once again to combine. Refrigerate until the cupcakes are cool and ready to ice.

5 Ice when the cupcakes are cold, with the help of a small knife or spatula.

TRUST ME TIPS

• Don't worry if the icing curdles when you add the orange juice. It will come right and give up the tantrum when you add the final batch of icing sugar. If for whatever reason it doesn't quite right itself, simply add more sugar until it has calmed down and is unified again.

Dollops of Cream

THERE ARE A HANDFUL OF RECIPES in this book that call for cream-based fillings. In order not to clutter up the recipe pages with too many ingredients and words, here they all are gathered together on one tidy page.

SERVES 8–10
AS A CAKE
ACCOMPANIMENT

**CRÈME À
L'ARMAGNAC**
200g crème fraîche
2 tbsp Armagnac
2 tbsp golden icing
  sugar, sieved

CRÈME AU RHUM
200g crème fraîche
2 tbsp rum
2 tbsp golden icing
  sugar, sieved

**CRÈME AU
CALVADOS**
200g crème fraîche
2 tbsp Calvados
2 tbsp golden icing
  sugar, sieved

**ORANGE BLOSSOM
CLOUD CREAM**
284ml double cream
1 tbsp icing sugar
1 tsp orange blossom
  water

VANILLA CREAM
284ml double cream
2 tbsp icing sugar,
  sieved
1 tsp vanilla extract

•   When beating crème fraîche with any other ingredient, always use a spoon, and a medium-sized bowl. You're really only mixing the ingredients together to incorporate them. It is absolutely vital to always use sieved icing sugar, if you wish to avoid any lumps . . .

•   By contrast, when beating double or whipping cream, you are hoping to lighten the texture of the cream with air, which is why you will need either an electric or a balloon whisk. The only really important aspects to remember when whipping cream are:

•   Always use fresh cream. Cream that has been left out of the fridge for even a couple of hours will whip and then become grainy within only a few minutes.

•   Be cautious when whipping cream, in order to avoid pushing it too far and encouraging it to become too stiff. If you reach this upsetting point, I'm afraid that the only thing left to do is to start all over again.

TRUST ME TIPS

•   All these delicate little ideas work just as well with half-fat crème fraîche if you are feeling the pinch. They will come out looser (as will your belt!) in texture, but the flavour will only alter slightly, becoming a fraction more acidic.

•   If you want to thicken the texture of one of these creams that you deem to be too loose, simply add more sieved icing sugar, a little at a time.

Cake Diaries

BIRTHDAY CAKE

Testing Number 1: 17 August

I'm rather hoping to get a finished recipe for this one by the end of the day and I like its atmosphere already. It's the answer to my Post-it note idea that said simply 'courgette and lemon'. It also has an awful lot of promise and balloon factor since it will be *my* own birthday cake, for my twenty-eighth birthday tomorrow. I think that Dolly Mixtures, hundreds and thousands and little gold balls encapsulate what I feel. Fingers crossed . . . Oh, it's perfect! I love the flavour and I love the texture. Thank you! Now this really is a birthday present. I'm off to print up the results.

SHARPIE STRAWBERRY JAM

Testing Number 1: 14 August

Wow, I love the smell of strawberries! Hoping for a sharp finish . . . Oh dear, it might just be a bit too sharp. I'll wait until it's cold. . . This jam is totally Mummy!

Testing Number 3: 16 August

This is a winner and it's to go into the middle of a brand-new friend called Birthday Cake.

CHOCOLATE CHOCOLATE CHIP CUPCAKES

Testing Number 1: 30 October

Damned nearly perfect the first time for these irresistible cheeky creatures! Will retest with less flour and cocoa powder and more carrot. Flavour is terrific!

Testing Number 2: 4 November

I think these have arrived where they were meant to go. Good news!

LEMON DROPS

Testing Number 1: 8 May

What I want is a lemon explosion (slightly wet and very sharp). This first mixture is very liquid – a very volatile and insecure consistency. Not convinced about swede, to be honest . . . These are not as chronic as I had first thought although they are clearly too wet. I need to up the amounts of almonds and flour by 10g each.

Testing Number 2: 8 May

It's funny/infuriating how a small and innocent little drop such as this could be quite so ferocious in its resistance to succeed!

Testing Number 3: 6 June

This return to Lemon Drops is a failiure! Why won't they behave? They're so small, yet so wilful. This is exasperating.

Testing Number 6: 28 October

I'm convinced that just like horses, they could smell fear and gleefully took advantage. After all this time coaxing and coercing, they are finally tame enough to pin down for the time it takes to quickly gobble one up. Thank goodness for that.

AUGUST WEDDING
CAKE

AUGUST WEDDING CAKE

THIS IS A DAY for home-made cake, full of hope and holding hands. The two floors of the cake are as strong as a home, and it's covered in real flowers from the garden because it's August and they're dying to be admired.

SERVES 80

Preparation time:
    1 hour per tier
Cooking time:
    1 hour per tier
Assembling time:
    2 hours

FOR THE FIRST TIER

6 medium free-range
    eggs
200g caster sugar
400g peeled and
    finely grated
    carrot
400g peeled and
    finely grated
    courgette
finely grated zest of
    8 juicing oranges
200g white rice flour
400g ground almonds
5 tsp baking powder
½ tsp salt
200ml elderflower
    cordial

FOR THE SECOND TIER

6 medium free-range
    eggs
200g caster sugar
400g peeled and finely
    grated carrot

INGREDIENTS
CONTINUED
OVERLEAF

1 Carefully pin the coloured ribbon round the edges of both cake boards and set them aside.

2 Preheat the oven to 180°C/350°F/gas mark 4.

3 Brush both the tins all over with a little oil before lining them with baking parchment. Cut into the corners with scissors and rearrange the parchment so that you end up with sharp square corners rather than scrunched-up paper. Finally, brush the parchment all over with a little oil and set aside.

4 Beat the eggs and the sugar for the first tier for 10 minutes until they have tripled in volume. Don't be suprised that they don't fluff up as much as smaller quantities do.

5 Add the grated carrot, courgette and orange zest before beating again until everything is well mixed. Finally, add the flour, ground almonds, baking powder, salt and the elderflower cordial, then mix until fully incorporated.

6 Pour the mixture into the larger tin and place it in the middle of the oven for **one hour**. Once cooked, remove the cake from the oven, unmould and cool on a wire rack while you make the second tier, repeating the instructions for the first.

7 To make the third tier, use the same method as above but with the altered ingredient quantities shown overleaf and the smaller tin.

8 Once the three cake tiers are cooked and cold, slice each of the cakes in half horizontally with a bread knife. You are now looking at six cake squares, four of which are big and two of which are smaller.

9 To make the icing, whisk the butter in a large mixing bowl with 3 tsp of the icing sugar until soft and pale. At the very beginning, the mixture will look like breadcrumbs. This is normal, and you should push on through this stage until the mixture is more unified, paler and fluffier than at first. Once the butter is relaxed and has completely absorbed the sugar, add another 4 tablespoons of icing sugar, along with a drizzle of the cordial, and whisk to incorporate.

CONTINUED OVERLEAF

400g peeled and
    finely grated
    courgette
finely grated zest of
    8 juicing oranges
200g white rice flour
400g ground almonds
5 tsp baking powder
½ tsp salt
200ml elderflower
    cordial

**FOR THE THIRD
TIER**
4 medium free-range eggs
150g caster sugar
300g peeled and finely
    grated carrot
300g peeled and finely
    grated courgette
finely grated zest of
    6 juicing oranges
150g white rice flour
300g ground almonds
4 tsp baking powder
¼ tsp salt
150ml elderflower cordial

FOR THE ICING
400g unsalted butter,
    at room temperature
1.75kg icing sugar,
    sieved
300ml elderflower cordial

TO DECORATE
fresh white flowers –
    roughly 160 stems

YOU WILL NEED
a 26cm-square x 9cm-
    deep loose-bottomed
    tin
a 20cm-square x 8cm-
    deep loose-bottomed
    tin

10 Continue with this process of adding the sugar and cordial, little by little, until both are all used up. To prevent the mixture from splitting, only add more sugar and cordial when the preceding amounts have been assimilated by the butter. If the icing starts to become grainy or too loose, simply add as little or as much sugar as is needed to bring it back to its unified self. Keep the finished icing at room temperature to make the icing process easier.

ASSEMBLING THE CAKE

Once you have the three cooked cakes that are all tidily cut through the middle to make six squares of cake, and all the icing made up and slightly soft, you are ready to assemble the wedding cake. You should mentally divide the icing into four equal parts. You can actually do this by splitting it into four smaller bowls if it helps you to make sense of the next steps (I always do).

1 Sandwich two of the larger square cakes together with the first portion of icing, and place this on to the bigger of the two cake boards.

2 Add another layer of icing and place another of the larger layers of cake on top. You will now have three layers of cake and two layers of icing.

3 Add one more layer of icing, followed by another layer of cake. You will now have used up all of the larger squares of cake and three of your bowls of icing.

4 Sandwich the two smaller squares of cake together with the final portion of icing sugar and place on the smaller cake board.

5 You are now ready to assemble the whole cake and decorate it with flowers. Place the smaller cake on top of the larger one, in the centre.

6 Now comes the fun bit! Cut the flower stems so that they are around 4cm long and plant them into the cake, covering all visible surfaces. It helps to make the cake look tidy if you opt for a well-structured flower head, such as a daisy or a rose, and if you stick to one variety and colour. Avoid tulips, as they wilt extremely quickly. It will also help the cake to look tidy if you plant rows of flowers, starting at the bottom, rather than position them willy-nilly.

7 To serve, remove the flowers and cut the cake into chunky little squares of two layers of cake and one layer of icing.

a 26cm-square cake
    board
a 20cm-square cake
    board
approx. 2m yellow
    ribbon 1.5cm wide
    (this gives you a
    little extra in case
    of emergency)
16 dressmaking pins
an extremely large
    mixing bowl (35cm
    diameter is ideal)
an electric hand whisk
a healthy dose of
    enthusiasm

• Don't worry if the raw cake mixture looks a bit lumpy and messy – mine does too. All the ugliness will be cooked out of it – that's a promise!

• If possible, once you have iced between the layers, it's a good idea to keep the assembled cakes in the fridge. The icing will benefit from being as chilled as possible before the flower-planting stage begins.

• This is a good time-saving tip but only applies to fan ovens in order to ensure the cakes cook evenly. Cook the first tier on its own, but you can cook the second and third tiers together (providing you prepare the mixtures simultaneously and don't let them sit). Place the the larger second tier on the top shelf of the oven and the smaller third tier on the bottom.

• You can either make up each batch of cake mixture while the previous one is in the oven, or make one cake every so often and freeze it. If freezing, I advise you to wrap each layer of cake individually and allow 24 hours for defrosting. Once defrosted, simply ice between the layers and proceed in the usual way.

VICTORIA SPONGE

IT'S A BRIGHT lemon day in early June and the cake stalls are all laid out behind the vicar's house. This cake is young and shy, with a perfectly ironed apron on, and her hair neatly plaited down her back. Although she would be mortified for anyone to suspect this, she is secretly hoping to win first prize, which is why her chest is slightly puffed up with pride.

SERVES 8

3 medium free-range
    eggs
150g caster sugar
200g peeled and finely
    grated potato (such
    as Maris Piper or
    King Edward)
100g white rice flour
2 tsp baking powder
¼ tsp salt
1 tsp vanilla extract

FOR THE FILLING

40g unsalted butter,
    cold and cubed
90g icing sugar,
    sieved (I like golden)
1 tsp boiling water
1 vanilla pod, split
    lengthways and the
    seeds scraped out
small pinch of salt
150g Sharpie Strawberry
    Jam (see page 7)
    or good-quality
    shop-bought jam

FOR THE TOP

a little caster sugar

YOU WILL NEED

two 18cm-diameter
    x 5cm-deep loose-
    bottomed tins

1 Preheat the oven to 180°C/350°F/gas mark 4. Lightly oil the base and sides of the tins. Place a circle of baking parchment over the base of each one and lightly oil this too.

2 Whisk the eggs and sugar together until pale, fluffy and tripled in volume. Whisk in the grated potato, followed by the flour, baking powder, salt and vanilla extract. Make sure everything is well combined.

3 Pour the mixture evenly into the two tins and place in the oven for **20 minutes** until the cakes are risen, golden and cooked all the way through. Unmould them on to a wire rack, peel off the parchment and set them aside to cool for 20 minutes whilst you make the filling.

4 To make the filling, whisk up the butter with an electric whisk until paste-like. Beat in the sugar one tablespoon at a time until it is all used up. Add the boiling water and whisk to combine. Add the vanilla seeds and salt, and beat again until fully incorporated.

5 Ice the bottom of one of the cold cakes. Cover the other cake bottom with strawberry jam before sandwiching the two together and dusting the top with caster sugar.

PASSIONFRUIT AND POMEGRANATE JELLY

THIS IS THE JELLY VERSION of those wonderful old-school ice lollies that look like rockets . . . This jelly is *fun*; it's playful food at its most jolly.

SERVES 8

FOR THE YELLOW LAYER

500ml water

150g caster sugar

9 leaves of gelatine

8 passionfruit, cut in half (the pulp should make roughly 300ml)

FOR THE RED LAYER

100ml water

3 leaves of gelatine

300ml pomegranate juice (from 2 large pomegranates or 4 small ones)

YOU WILL NEED

8 pretty glasses or individual glass bowls

1 Heat the water and sugar for the yellow layer gently until the sugar has completely dissolved. This won't take more than 3 or 4 minutes and won't require the water to boil. Let this mixture stand.

2 Meanwhile, place the gelatine leaves in a small bowl and cover them completely with cold water. Let them stand for approximately 3 minutes, then wring the gelatine out in your hands and pop it into the hot sugary water to dissolve. Swish it around the pan a few times to make sure that it has all disintegrated before adding the passionfruit pulp.

3 Give the mixture a good stir with a spoon, then ladle or pour the juice into the serving glasses, distributing the mixture evenly between all eight. Place them in the fridge and leave to set for 3 hours or overnight at room temperature.

4 Once the yellow layer is set, turn your attention to the red (much thinner) layer of jelly. Heat the water in a small pan until it gets hot but not too hot – you should be able to put your finger comfortably into the water. Whilst you heat the water, soak the gelatine leaves in the pomegranate juice to soften. Once limp between your fingers, place the leaves in the hot water and stir to dissolve. When they have all disappeared, mix in the pomegranate juice.

5 Remove the glasses of set passionfruit jelly from the fridge and spoon the pomegranate mixture evenly over the yellow layer in each one. Refrigerate once more for 2 hours to set before serving.

TRUST ME TIPS

• The gelatine that can be found in shops has changed in the last five years. One leaf of gelatine used to be enough to set an entire mousse or bavarois, but now it can take twelve leaves to set 1 litre! Still, whatever brand of gelatine you use, simply follow the instructions on the packet and you will be fine. I prefer mine to be on the lighter side, as I think that very tough jelly is totally horrid.

PEACH AND POPPY SEED MUFFINS

THESE BREAKFAST NUMBERS are stuffed with slow-release energy, and are the perfect beginning to a hectic day.

MAKES 9

2 medium free-range
  eggs
120g caster sugar
200g peeled and finely
  grated sweet
  potato
100g white rice flour
100g ground almonds
1 tbsp poppy seeds
2 tsp baking powder
½ tsp bicarbonate of soda
¼ tsp salt
3 small peaches cut into
  ½-cm cubes

YOU WILL NEED

a 12-hole muffin tray
9 muffin cases (see
  page xxvii for exact
  size)

1 Preheat the oven to 180°C/350°F/gas mark 4 and line the muffin tray with the paper cases.

2 Whisk the eggs and caster sugar for 3 minutes until fluffy. With the help of a wooden spoon, beat in the grated sweet potato, flour, ground almonds, poppy seeds, baking powder, bicarbonate of soda and salt until well incorporated.

3 Fold in the cubes of peach, then fill the cases right up to the top.

4 Bake in the oven for **30 minutes** until risen and golden.

5 Remove from the oven and cool on a wire rack.

TRUST ME TIPS

• It is very important to the sudden rise of a muffin that you don't overbeat the mixture before putting it into the cases.

• I often use tinned peaches as the peach season is so short.

WHITE CHOCOLATE, CINNAMON AND RASPBERRY BLONDIE

THIS SQUIDGY SQUARE is sitting with the top two buttons of his trousers undone, so full and lazy is he from his lunch. He knew that having another helping was pushing it, but he thought that he could cheat *just this once* and get away with it . . .

SERVES 9

3 medium free-range
   eggs
120g caster sugar
250g peeled and finely
   grated butternut
   squash
50g white rice flour
100g ground almonds
1 tsp cinnamon
2 tsp baking powder
¼ tsp salt
150g fresh raspberries
100g white chocolate,
   chopped into small
   chunks

FOR THE TOP
30g flaked almonds
a little icing sugar

YOU WILL NEED
a 22cm-square x 5cm-
   deep brownie tin

1 Preheat the oven to 200°C/400°F/gas mark 6. Line the base and sides of your tin with baking parchment. A big square placed over the top is enough; you then cut into each corner to make a neat pleat. It's also a good idea to dot a tiny bit of oil on the base and sides of the tin to help the parchment stick down. Once it is in place, lightly brush the parchment on the base and sides with a little vegetable oil.

2 Beat the eggs and sugar in a large mixing bowl for 5 minutes until pale, fluffy and quadrupled in volume – I mean a big bouffant hairstyle for this one! Add the grated butternut squash and beat again. Add the flour, ground almonds, cinnamon, baking powder and salt. Beat until well incorporated.

3 Pour half the mixture into the prepared tin and scatter over it the raspberries and the chocolate chunks. Cover with the remaining mixture.

4 Sprinkle the flaked almonds over the cake and place it in the top of the oven for **25 minutes** until just cooked.

5 Cool the blondie in the tin for 20 minutes, then sieve a little icing sugar over the top before cutting it into individual squares and serving.

STEM GINGER SYRUP CAKE

THERE IS NO EDGE to this cake. All she wants is to soothe and be kind.

SERVES 12

3 medium free-range
  eggs
120g Demerara sugar
250g peeled and very
  finely grated
  butternut squash
30g piece raw ginger,
  peeled and very
  finely grated
150g white rice flour
100g ground almonds
1 tsp ground ginger
2 tsp baking powder
¼ tsp salt
4 tbsp stem ginger syrup
100g stem ginger, very
  finely sliced

FOR THE TOP

3 tbsp stem ginger syrup
100g golden icing sugar,
  sieved
3 knobs stem ginger,
  very finely sliced

YOU WILL NEED

a 23cm-diameter x
  7cm-deep loose-
  bottomed tin

1 Preheat the oven to 180°C/350°F/gas mark 4. Line the base of the tin with baking parchment, then lightly brush all over the parchment and the sides of the tin with a little vegetable oil.

2 Whisk the eggs and sugar in a large mixing bowl until pale and four times their original volume (roughly 5 minutes on full blast). Whisk in the grated butternut squash and raw ginger until all mixed in. Next, add the flour, ground almonds, ground ginger, baking powder and salt, and beat again until well incorporated.

3 Use a spatula to fold in the ginger syrup and the slices of stem ginger so that they are dotted around the place. Pour the mixture into the tin and place it in the middle of the oven for **30 minutes.**

4 Remove the cake from the oven and allow it to cool in the tin for 10 minutes before unmoulding on to a wire rack. Peel the parchment from the bottom and flip the cake the right way up again to avoid making lines on the top.

5 Make the icing by mixing together the stem ginger syrup with the sieved icing sugar. Dot the slices of stem ginger over the surface of the cake and pour the icing over before serving.

TRUST ME TIPS

• The raw ginger is pretty difficult to grate finely because it is so stringy. If you find this stage one step too far down the road of faff, just replace it with another teaspoon of ground ginger to produce a little extra flavour.

• With Demerara or other coarse sugars, it is really important to beat long enough to blend them in completely, as you need to sand down the crystals until they have disappeared and are stabilizing the air in the egg whites. Overlooking or underestimating this stage will affect the texture and rise of the whole cake.

HONEY AND SUNFLOWER GINGER SCONES

THESE PERKY LITTLE SCONES are a choir of happy children. Ginger is the best kind of teacher, Carrot is over-excited at the organ, whilst Honey and the Sunflower Seeds are sitting in the side wings, watching on with pride and cartons of juice.

MAKES 10

220g white spelt flour, plus a little extra for rolling and dusting
1 tbsp ground ginger
2 tsp baking powder
½ tsp bicarbonate of soda
½ tsp salt
200g topped, tailed, peeled and super-finely grated carrot
30g unsalted butter, cold and cubed
25g piece raw ginger, peeled and finely grated
2 tbsp clear honey, such as orange blossom
3 tbsp sunflower seeds
a little milk

YOU WILL NEED

a 6cm pastry-cutter
a food processor

1 Preheat the oven to 200°C/400°F/gas mark 6 and line a baking sheet with foil and baking parchment. Lightly dust the parchment with flour.

2 Put the flour, ginger, baking powder, bicarbonate of soda and salt into the bowl of a food processor, followed by the grated carrot, butter, raw ginger and honey. Give it a few good pulses, until the mixture starts coming together. Add the sunflower seeds before pulsing again to combine.

3 Tip the scone mixture on to a lightly floured surface, and roll out very delicately to roughly 4cm thick.

4 Cut out ten circles and place them on the prepared baking sheet. It's important to make sure that the scones all have a dusting of flour on their bottoms to prevent them from sticking to the baking parchment.

5 Brush with a little milk and sprinkle a little flour over them before placing into the top of the oven for **17–19 minutes**. You know when they're ready because they will look all risen and sunny – and your kitchen will smell of gingerbread men.

TRUST ME TIPS

• Please, please, please, when it comes to scones, do not press down hard on them when rolling them out – they hate pressure of any kind. If you think that you can bully them into working, you are mistaken, as they will simply refuse to rise. Treat the dough with kindness and feather-like care when you handle it. This is ballerina stuff, not boxing.

CONTINUED OVERLEAF

•   You will get eight pretty, slightly smug, perfect scones. The last two, which you may have to re-roll from the leftover ends of the original dough, will doubtless have more character and be a bit wonky. This just means that they're a bit more special than the rest and should be kept back for special occasions or favourite uncles.

•   These scones are just perfect with Bonfire Blackcurrant Jam (see pages 55–6) or apricot jam . . . and clotted cream, of course.

LEMON AND CINNAMON BARLEY WATER

THIS RECIPE IS a liquid Florence Nightingale, with a kind word and a clean handkerchief when you feel under the weather. Drink either hot (with a tot of bourbon), or chilled in the summer as it is. It's quite the opposite to 'barley waters' that are full of fake colours and hysterical flavours.

MAKES 1.4 LITRES

100g pearl barley
finely grated zest and
    juice of 4 unwaxed
    lemons
4 cinnamon sticks
2.4 litres water
120g caster sugar

YOU WILL NEED

one or more glass
    bottle(s) with lid(s)

1 Preheat the oven to 100°C/200°F/gas mark ¼. Place the bottle, with its lid separately, in the oven to sterilize. Remove just before using. Don't worry if the liquid sizzles a bit as you pour it into the bottle – this is quite normal.

2 Rinse the barley under the tap to wash off the excess starch. Put the lemon zest into a large saucepan along with the rinsed barley and cinnamon sticks. Add the water and bring to the boil.

3 Simmer the mixture on very low for 1 hour. If you look into the pan, the odd rogue shred of lemon zest should be rolling lazily to the surface, like slow-motion yellow feathers somersaulting upwards. Anything more energetic than this will evaporate too much water, which will over-concentrate and wreck the barley water.

4 Strain the mixture through a sieve, discarding the zest and barley. Add the sugar. Stir to dissolve for a minute or so until no sugar crystals are left.

5 Strain the lemon juice (which should come to roughly 240ml) through a sieve and add to the hot liquid. Pour into the bottle and add the cinnamon sticks before sealing the top. Store in the fridge until needed. Dilute one part barley water to one part water.

TRUST ME TIPS

• The level of simmering is really important since it will dictate how intense or mild the barley involvement is in this recipe. Added to which, if you boil the liquid too hard for an hour, you will expel any reparative qualities of this drink by boiling out the goodness.

COURGETTE AND CAMOMILE CUPCAKES

BRING OUT THE RUG and a bottle of cold lemonade because it's that glorious time of year again . . . English summer.

MAKES 12

2 medium free-range
    eggs
120g caster sugar
finely grated zest of ½
    lemon
200g topped, tailed,
    peeled and finely
    grated courgette
5 camomile tea bags
150g white rice flour
50g ground almonds
2 tsp baking powder
½ tsp bicarbonate of soda
¼ tsp salt

FOR THE ICING

3 tbsp strong camomile
    tea (use 1 tea bag
    and 100ml boiling
    water)
2 tbsp freshly squeezed
    lemon juice
160g icing sugar, sieved

YOU WILL NEED

a 12-hole muffin tray
12 cupcake cases (see
    page xxvii for exact
    size)

1 Preheat the oven to 180°C/350°F/gas mark 4. Line the muffin tray with the paper cases.

2 In a medium-sized mixing bowl, whisk the eggs and sugar for 3 minutes until fluffy and pale. First add the lemon zest and courgette, and give it all a whisk until fully incorporated. Next tip the camomile out of its tea bags (it comes out as a fine powder) into the egg and honey mixture, and add the flour, ground almonds, baking powder, bicarbonate of soda and salt.

3 Once all are well mixed in together, ladle the mixture evenly into the cupcake cases so that it comes four fifths of the way up the sides. Bake for **30 minutes** while you make the icing.

4 To make the icing, mix the camomile tea and lemon juice with the icing sugar in a small bowl until you reach a white paste-like consistency. If not using the icing until later, place a sheet of cling film directly on to the surface to prevent it drying out.

5 Remove the cupcakes from the oven and cool on a wire rack for 15 minutes. Ice each cupcake with the help of a spoon.

TRUST ME TIPS

• Dipping a teaspoon into the leftover tea and using the back of it as a spatula makes icing the cupcakes easier.

LIGHT CHOCOLATE CAKE

DESPITE BEING ON THE COVER of the book, this cake is shy. But she's going to have to learn how to handle the attention; she's too stunning and scrumptious not to be noticed.

SERVES 12

3 medium free-range
    eggs
160g caster sugar
200g peeled and grated
    butternut squash
120g white rice flour
3 tbsp good-quality
    cocoa powder
80g ground almonds
1 tsp baking powder
1 tsp bicarbonate of soda
¼ tsp salt
125ml buttermilk

FOR THE ICING

50g unsalted butter,
    softened
200g icing sugar, sieved
50g mascarpone
4 tsp cocoa powder
small pinch of salt

FOR THE TOP

handful of spray roses
    (with stems at least
    2cm long)

YOU WILL NEED

two 18cm-diameter x
    5cm-deep loose-
    bottomed tins

1 Preheat the oven to 180°C/350°F/gas mark 4. Line the tins with baking parchment and brush a little vegetable oil over the base and sides.

2 Whisk the eggs and sugar in a large mixing bowl for 4 full minutes until pale and fluffy. Beat in the grated butternut squash, followed by the flour, cocoa powder, ground almonds, baking powder, bicarbonate of soda and salt. Add the buttermilk before beating again one last time to make sure that all the ingredients are well introduced to one another.

3 Pour the mixture evenly into both tins, then place in the middle of the oven for **30 minutes**.

4 Once cooked, remove the cakes from the oven, unmould, peel off the baking parchment and leave them to cool down completely on a wire rack.

5 You can make the icing whilst the cakes are cooking, as long as you don't ice them until they are completely cold, otherwise the icing will run off. Beat the butter with 100g of the sugar in a large mixing bowl. You will need to work them together patiently, using the back of a wooden spoon. It will seem like an impossible task at first, but they will eventually turn into a lovely rich paste.

6 Once you reach this stage, beat vigorously for 10 seconds to loosen the butter even further. Add the mascarpone, cocoa powder and salt, as well as the remaining sugar. Beat once again to combine.

7 Refrigerate the icing for 15 minutes. Give it a good beating with your wooden spoon before icing the middle and top of the cold cake. Decorate the top with flowers before serving.

Cake Diaries

PEACH AND POPPY SEED MUFFINS

Testing Number 1: 28 May

I haven't been in the kitchen for about a week and these little poppets are just the sort of people that make it fun to come back. I envisage them to be exactly the kind of children you might hope your kids will make friends with in the playground. Totally uncool, completely reliable and without malice. This would be a great breakfast number with fruit and slow-releasing veg. Not a bad first attempt.

WHITE CHOCOLATE, CINNAMON AND RASPBERRY BLONDIE

Testing Number 1: 2 September

It's funny, this cake seems quite exhausted. I'm seeking to jazz him up a bit with some white choc and pumpkin (instead of swede – have gone off swede completely). It would help if I hadn't forgotten the blinking baking powder. What a clot I am. Now *I'm* feeling lethargic!

Testing Number 3: 10 September

I'm hoping that he is going to come alive this time . . .

Testing Number 4: 11 November

It's Armistice Day today and I mustn't forget to keep from chattering to the cakes for 1 minute at 11 a.m. (roughly 6 minutes from now). I'm especially hopeful today . . . Ooh, yum! Touchdown! He's so light and wonderful!

STEM GINGER SYRUP CAKE

Testing Number 1: 25 November

This divine and graceful cake embodies generosity. She landed into existence with a gentle soft thud. You're wonderful, Stem Ginger Syrup Cake. Unimprovable.

COURGETTE AND CAMOMILE CUPCAKES

Testing Number 1: 10 April

From now on courgette = top student and favourite cake friend. This was a hole-in-one. And to think that I always considered courgette to be a bitter type!

Testing Number 2: 12 April

I'm very happy with this flavour, especially now that I've introduced a little lemon and camomile into the icing. Rosemary will be pleased: this one has such a great personality.

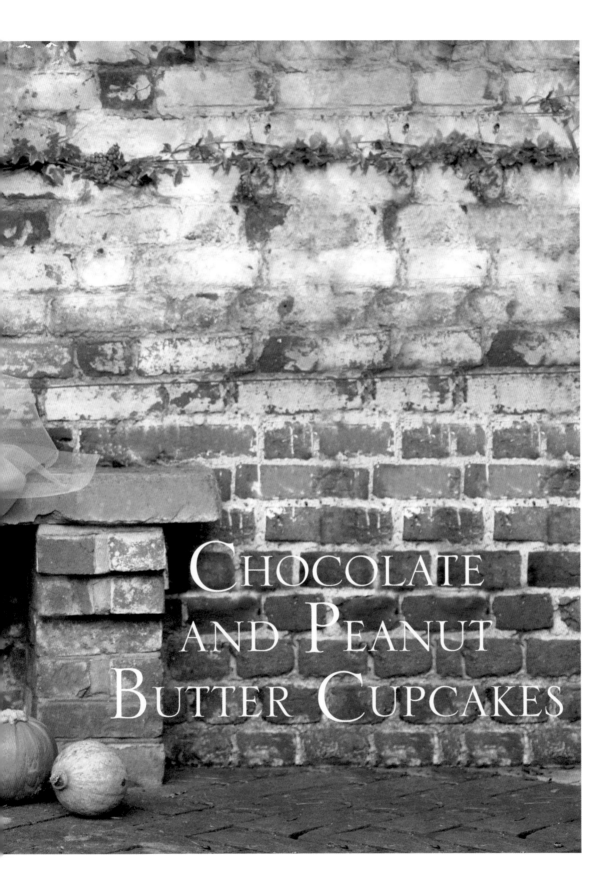

CHOCOLATE AND PEANUT BUTTER CUPCAKES

CHOCOLATE AND PEANUT BUTTER CUPCAKES

THIS IS THE CUPCAKE that translates that photograph of your sister or son, who, aged two and a half, is hiding in a corner of the birthday party with chocolate smeared *all over* their face. It's the sharp shock when they look up from their chocolate universe, with a mixture of surprise and 'Go away' . . .

MAKES 12

100g unsalted peanuts
3 medium free-range eggs
200g light Muscovado
    sugar
200g peeled and finely
    grated **pumpkin**
    (or **butternut**
    squash)
100g white rice flour
40g best-quality cocoa
    powder
2 tsp baking powder
¼ tsp salt

FOR THE ICING

60g smooth peanut butter
2 tbsp golden icing
    sugar, sieved
2 tbsp cocoa powder
pinch of salt
5 tbsp boiling water

FOR THE TOP

small handful of roughly
    chopped peanuts,
    or some grated dark
    chocolate

YOU WILL NEED

a 12-hole muffin tray
12 cupcake cases (see page
    xxvii for exact size)
a food processor

1 Preheat the oven to 180°C/350°F/gas mark 4. Line the muffin tray with the paper cases.

2 Blitz the peanuts in the food processor until totally ground; as well as being pulverized to a powder, make sure that they are evenly ground. Set aside.

3 Whisk the eggs and sugar for 5 minutes until pale coffee coloured and fluffy. Next, whisk in the grated pumpkin, followed by the flour, cocoa powder, baking powder, salt and ground peanuts. Whisk until all the ingredients are well combined.

4 Spoon the mixture into the paper cases so that it comes four fifths of the way up the sides, then place in the middle of the oven for **30 minutes**.

5 Remove the cakes from the oven and cool for 10 minutes in the tray, then transfer to the fridge and leave to cool completely.

6 To make the icing, mix the peanut butter, icing sugar, cocoa powder and salt with the back of a spoon to form a paste. Next, slowly and gently incorporate the boiling water with a balloon whisk, one spoonful at a time. You will end up with a smooth and delicious paste. Ice the cupcakes when completely cold, and decorate with a little grated chocolate or some roughly chopped extra peanuts.

TRUST ME TIPS

• If you can't be bothered to blitz the peanuts in a food processor (or if you don't have one), simply replace them with ground almonds.

ORANGE AND CARDAMOM STEAMED SPONGE

THIS WINTER PUDDING is a sofa that you sink into and never want to leave . . . Behind the taste of oranges is a daydream of elephants in India.

SERVES 10

finely grated zest of 2
    sharp-flavoured
    oranges (juicing
    varieties, such as
    Seville, are best)
15 cardamom pods
3 medium free-range
    eggs
200g granulated sugar
200g topped, tailed,
    peeled and finely
    grated **turnip**
150g white rice flour
50g ground almonds
2 tsp baking powder
¼ tsp salt

FOR THE BASE OF THE PUDDING (OPTIONAL BUT DELICIOUS)
2 tbsp clear honey
the rest of the 2 oranges

YOU WILL NEED
a really big saucepan
    (a stock pan is ideal)
a 2-litre pudding basin
a pestle and mortar
kitchen string

1 Put a full kettle of water on to boil.

2 Take a sheet of tin foil (about 30cm square) and another of baking parchment the same size. Place these sheets on top of each other with the parchment on the bottom. Make a pleat about 6cm wide in the middle of both layers, so that the two are pleated together and the steam can billow up into the pleat.

3 Grease the parchment side of this lid (which will be in contact with the surface of the pudding) and set aside for later.

4 Take another length of foil, roughly 40cm long. Fold it over itself, making a solid strip of foil roughly 8cm wide. Set aside.

5 Lightly grease the pudding basin. Pour the honey into the base of the basin. Finely grate the zest from the oranges and set this aside for later. Remove the skins and any remaining pith from the oranges by cutting around the globe, from pole to pole. Slice the 'bald' oranges into thin horizontal slices. Place them at the bottom of the pudding basin. Don't feel that you have to use them all up. I often use 4 slices and just eat the rest in an orange daydream as I'm cooking. Set aside until needed.

6 Using a pestle and mortar, bash up the cardamom pods a couple of times to loosen their shells. Remove the husky shell bits – this may be a hassle but does need to be done. Gently bash the seeds for another minute or so – 'gently' because they are naturally acrobatic and love nothing more than somersaulting out of the mortar and on to the floor. Don't expect dust, but uneven cardamom sand is just right here.

7 Whisk the eggs and sugar for 4 minutes until pale and full of airs and graces, before adding the grated turnip and orange zest and whisking for another minute. Finally, add the flour, ground almonds, baking powder and salt and whisk to combine.

8 Pour the mixture into the prepared basin and place the foil-and-paper 'hat' over the top, foil side up. Wrap the string twice around the lip of the basin, making sure you leave no gaps where water could get through.

9 Trim the parchment and foil layers carefully so that only a couple of centimetres are left below the string line. Any more and the water will catch and ride up inside the lid; any less and the steam inside the pudding will push the lid upwards and let the water in. Tie the string firmly with a knot to secure the lid.

10 Lower the basin into the saucepan with the help of your home-made length of foil, making sure that the basin sits squarely on top of the foil strip (so that taking it out is easy later on). Pour boiling water into the pan around your pudding (avoiding the top) until the water level reaches the lip. Turn on the heat so that you have a rolling simmer (slightly angry but not furious) before placing the lid over the saucepan.

11 After **1 hour 30 minutes**, remove the pudding with the help of the foil strip and set aside to cool for 10 minutes.

12 Serve with cardamom-infused Crème Anglaise (use 5 pods; see pages 50–1), or Orange Blossom Cloud Cream (see page 20).

TRUST ME TIPS

• The bottom of the pudding is in my view as fun as the present in a Kinder egg or the chocolate tip at the bottom of a Cornetto – which is why I recommend that you go to the bother of making the orange slices and honey syrup.

• I don't always have a pestle and mortar to hand, and find that a rolling pin and a solid pudding basin work just as well, providing that you put a tea towel under the basin to prevent it from shattering over the kitchen surface!

Sunken Apricot and Almond Cake

THIS CAKE HAILS from tatty, southern Spain: somewhere between heaven and the almond groves. The hills roll down to the sea and ring with the sound of cowbells.

SERVES 10

3 medium free-range
  eggs
180g caster sugar
200g peeled and finely
  grated **butternut
  squash**
1 tsp almond essence
60g white rice flour
200g ground almonds
2 tsp mixed spice
2 tsp baking powder
¼ tsp salt
240g tinned apricot
  halves in juice,
  drained

FOR THE TOP
generous dusting of
  icing sugar

YOU WILL NEED
a 23cm-diameter x
  7cm-deep loose-
  bottomed tin or ten
  8cm x 5cm-deep
  loose-bottomed
  fluted tart tins

1 Preheat the oven to 180°C/350°F/gas mark 4.

2 If you are using one large tin, simply line the base with baking parchment. Lightly grease the parchment and the sides of the tin. If you are using mini tart tins, don't bother lining them with baking parchment (life is just too short for this). Instead, make sure that you are thorough when it comes to brushing a little oil around the sides and the base. If your sides are fluted, go into the pipes thoroughly with the brush to avoid any sticking later on.

3 Whisk the eggs and sugar for 4 minutes until pale and fluffy. Add the grated butternut squash and the almond essence, then whisk briefly to combine.

4 Add the flour, ground almonds, mixed spice, baking powder and salt, then give it a final whisk to make sure that all the ingredients are well introduced to one another.

5 Pour this mixture into the prepared tin and place the apricots hither and thither in the cake batter, letting them sit as if cushioned by the mixture, which will puff up around them. If using individual tins, aim for up to two or three apricot halves per tartlet. Put in the middle of the oven and bake the big cake for **45 minutes** or the smaller ones for **35 minutes**.

6 Once cooked, remove from the oven and run a knife around the edge of the large tin. If you have used small fluted tins, simply insert the tip of a skewer or fork into each of the flutes and ease the cake away from the sides. In both cases, let the cake stand in the tin for 5 minutes to settle before sieving over the icing sugar.

7 Serve warm straight away or cold later on. This cake is delicious accompanied by apricot or almond ice cream.

CRÈME ANGLAISE

THIS LIGHT CUSTARD recipe is only designed for very patient people and thinkers. It requires you to shut out the world for quarter of an hour and concentrate on the contents of one small saucepan. If you're a daydreamer, this is your time to slip off and build castles in the air. Don't lose heart, you'll get there in the end.

**SERVES 6
(MAKES 500ML)**

600ml semi-
    skimmed milk
40g caster sugar
10 or so scratches
    of nutmeg
yolks of 4 medium
    free-range eggs

YOU WILL NEED

a flat-ended wooden
    spoon or spatula
a daydream to pass
    the time

1 Heat the milk in a small saucepan with the sugar and nutmeg until there is a slight heat haze over it, as well as a fine film of froth – this is *before* boiling point.

2 In a medium bowl, mix the egg yolks with the flat-ended wooden spoon to break them up. Very slowly (by which I mean only a thin trickle) pour the hot milk over this mixture and keep on mixing with the wooden spoon until all the milk is used up, then stir for a minute in the bowl.

3 Quickly wash the little pan and transfer the liquid back into it, then place over the lowest possible heat. Stir slowly and continuously for 15 minutes, making sure that you cover the base of the pan with your spoon so that none of the mixture ever sticks to the bottom or sides and overcooks. Your aim is to maintain the heat haze at the same point.

4 Once the 15 minutes are up and you have a yellow, silky-looking pan of slightly thick milk, transfer it to a cold jug and set aside to cool down a little. The custard shouldn't look too thick at this point (it shouldn't be like shop-bought custard), so don't be afraid that it isn't thick enough. Not only is it perfect as it is, but it wants 10 minutes in a jug on its own to settle down, become accustomed to its new self, and thicken to exactly the perfect point.

5 If using much later, transfer the jug of custard to the fridge once it is cool; otherwise serve it while it's still warm. Don't reheat for fear of overcooking the eggs.

TRUST ME TIPS

• It is best to make this on a gas hob, as it can be turned down very low. It is much harder to do this with induction heat or electric; they will make life much harder, I'm afraid.

- The flat-ended wooden spoon or spatula is crucial to the success of the recipe since it prevents any of this highly delicate mixture from sticking to the base or sides of the pan and overcooking.

- Making custard is a bit like herding sheep. If even a small fraction of the herd breaks away, they will all follow eventually and the whole pan will end up on the wrong side of the gate. Although tedious, it's because eggs and sheep are so similar that you need to wash out the pan before starting on the 15-minute daydream . . . Even the smallest particle of cooked egg will open that horrid gate and jeopardize the whole plan.

- The heat haze described opposite is just that – a warm mist over the surface of the milk, accompanied by a slight froth. If it ever changes appearance, it might well be an indication that the heat is too high and the mixture will curdle – so be aware of whom you're dealing with and take it off the heat immediately. If you do push it too quickly and curdle the custard, you will have to throw it away and start all over again in a clean saucepan. I've done this many times and it makes me want to cry every time I do it.

- This recipe is designed as a blueprint for a number of different flavoured custards. Whenever I have used it, I have slightly adapted or modified the Crème to match its pudding or cake surroundings. In each case, remember to add the flavouring (whether vanilla, cardamom, etc.) at the same point as the nutmeg in this recipe. This is the true blue beginning: Number One Crème Anglaise, from which all the others are made.

STEAMED GOLDEN SYRUP SPONGE PUDDING

THINK OF *The Secret Garden* and living at Misselthwaite Manor, under the vigilant eye of Mrs Medlock; skipping to keep warm and looking forward to tea and pudding . . .

SERVES 10

250g golden syrup, plus a further 3 tbsp for the base of the pudding
3 medium free-range eggs
250g topped, tailed, peeled and grated **turnip** (I use purple ones)
grated zest of 1 unwaxed lemon
150g white rice flour
50g ground almonds
2 tsp baking powder
¼ tsp salt

YOU WILL NEED

a really big saucepan (a stock pan is ideal)
a 2-litre pudding basin
kitchen string

1 Put a full kettle of water on to boil.

2 Take a sheet of tin foil (about 30cm square) and another of baking parchment the same size. Place these sheets on top of each other with the parchment on the bottom. Make a pleat about 6cm wide in the middle of both layers, so that the two are pleated together and the steam can billow up into the pleat. This will end up looking like a milkmaid's hat once it's safely on the pudding.

3 Grease the parchment side of this lid (which will be in contact with the surface of the pudding) and set aside for later.

4 Take another length of foil, roughly 40cm long. Fold it over itself, making a solid strip of foil roughly 8cm wide. Set aside.

5 Lightly grease the pudding basin. Pour the 3 tbsp of golden syrup into the base of the basin and set aside.

6 Beat the golden syrup and eggs for 4 minutes until bubbly and confident, before adding the grated turnip and lemon zest, whisking for another minute. Finally, add the flour, ground almonds, baking powder and salt, and whisk to combine.

7 Pour into the prepared basin and place the foil-and-paper milkmaid's hat over the top, foil side up. Wrap the string twice around the lip of the basin, making sure you leave no gaps where water could get through. Tie the string firmly with a knot to secure the lid.

8 Trim the parchment and foil layers carefully so that only a couple of centimetres are left below the string line. Any more and the water will catch and ride up inside the lid; any less and the steam inside the pudding will push the lid upwards and let the water in.

CONTINUED OVERLEAF

9 Lower the basin into the saucepan with the help of your home-made length of foil, making sure that the basin sits squarely on top of the foil strip (so that taking it out is extra easy later on).

10 Pour boiling water from the kettle into the pan around your pudding (avoiding the top) until the water level reaches the lip. Turn on the heat and bring to a rolling simmer (slightly angry but not furious) before placing the lid over the saucepan.

11 After **1 hour 30 minutes**, remove the pudding with the help of the foil strip and set aside to cool for 20 minutes.

12 This pudding is delicious served with Crème Anglaise. Follow the method on pages 50–1, only heat the milk with 40g golden syrup (as opposed to sugar) before pouring over the eggs.

TRUST ME TIPS

•   When making this recipe, it is really important to be prepared with all the pudding paraphernalia sorted out ahead of cooking.

•   Don't worry if the pudding only comes two thirds of the way up the bowl. This is deliberate and will enable it to rise correctly, keeping the pudding beautiful and light.

•   Don't forget to top up the water level in the pan, as it will evaporate as it goes along, even with a lid on. The water shouldn't fall below the lip of the basin, or the pudding won't cook evenly.

•   When opening up your pudding 'present', be careful of the steam, which burns with merciless heat even after sitting for a while.

•   If you are trying to be good or don't have time to make Crème Anglaise, a little single cream makes a lovely accompaniment instead (especially if you scratch a little nutmeg into it).

BONFIRE BLACKCURRANT JAM

SO BRIEF IS THE SEASON for these tiny purple beads that I would get up in the middle of the night with a torch to steal them . . . Perhaps it's the smell of bonfires in the air that makes me feel like Guy Fawkes himself.

MAKES 1.5 LITRES

900g **blackcurrants**
900ml water
900g jam sugar (with added pectin; also called preserving sugar)

YOU WILL NEED
four jam jars with lids
a really big saucepan or stock pan

1 Preheat the oven to 100°C/200°F/gas mark ¼.

2 Put the blackcurrants in a colander and rinse well under the tap. Bring the washed fruit and measured water to the boil in a large pan. Turn down the heat and simmer gently for 40 minutes uncovered, until quite soft.

3 After 20 minutes of the fruit softening on the hob, spread the sugar over a clean baking sheet and place in the hot oven for 20 minutes.

4 Once the sugar is warmed, remove it from the oven and replace with the jam jars, with their lids separately. Putting them into the oven sterilizes them and warms them so that the glass doesn't crack under the pressure of the hot jam. Remove the jars from the oven after 10 minutes of warming.

5 Meanwhile, add the warmed sugar (it smells deliciously of candyfloss) to the saucepan. Stir on the low heat that the pan is already sitting over until the sugar has dissolved – this takes 5 minutes or so. Once there are no little gritty crystals of sugar under your spoon, bring to the boil. Boil fast for 10 minutes. Remember to stir the jam all the time, covering the base of the pan and right into the corners. This will prevent any sticking and burning. Spoon off any light-coloured scum that appears on the surface.

6 Spoon the jam carefully into the hot jars and put their lids on tightly. Leave to cool for an hour before tasting.

TRUST ME TIPS

• To prepare the fruit before washing, simply pluck the blackcurrants from their thin stems and drop them into a colander. There's no need to worry about the little bunny tails, as they are perfectly harmless and, in fact, I quite like the occasional small soft bite in the jam.

CONTINUED OVERLEAF

• It is important not to put the heat up straight after adding the warm sugar, as it can crystallize if not handled with care; hence the instruction to dissolve the granules before heating to a fast boil.

• When making any sort of jam, it is really important to keep your eye on the saucepan, especially after the sugar has gone into the stewed fruit. A sort of fruity caramel will try with all its might to escape from the top if you're not careful. If this happens, it means that either your saucepan isn't big enough or that the jam is getting too hot – either problem can be solved by turning down the heat.

• For an easy dessert that is completely delicious, serve Bonfire Blackcurrant Jam over vanilla ice cream and with a few toasted almonds sprinkled over it.

MISS MARPLE SEED CAKE

THE THING ABOUT Miss Marple is that she is utterly reliable. You know from the minute she appears at a crime scene that she will track down the criminal with steely determination and ruthless wit. She once deplored the absence of *real* seed cake on the tea menu at Bertram's Hotel. This recipe is for you, Miss Marple.

SERVES 10

3 medium free-range
    eggs
160g caster sugar, plus
    a little extra for
    dusting
½ tsp salt
240g peeled and finely
    grated floury **potato**
    (Maris Piper is good)
100g white rice flour
50g ground almonds
2 tsp baking powder
1 heaped tbsp caraway
    seeds
½ tsp grated nutmeg
1 tsp ground mace
    (optional)
2 tbsp brandy

YOU WILL NEED

an 18cm-diameter x
    5cm-deep loose-
    bottomed tin

1 Preheat the oven to 180°C/350°F/gas mark 4 and line the base of the tin with baking parchment. Lightly brush the parchment and sides of the tin with a little vegetable oil.

2 In a large mixing bowl whisk together the eggs, sugar and salt until they have doubled in volume and look the colour of custard – this takes roughly 5 minutes' solid whisking and is a really important stage that shouldn't be overlooked!

3 Add the grated potato before whisking again to combine. Add the flour, ground almonds, baking powder, caraway seeds, grated nutmeg, ground mace (if using) and brandy before briefly whisking one last time.

4 Pour the mixture into the prepared tin and place in the middle of the oven for **40 minutes**.

5 Remove the cake from the oven, unmould it and cool on a wire rack. Dust the top with caster sugar and serve. Store in an airtight container.

TRUST ME TIPS

• I highly recommend grating your own nutmeg, as the flavour is about twelve times better than the ready-ground stuff.

• The top of the cake should vaguely resemble crumpets. Don't be alarmed when you take it out of the oven and it looks bubbly on the top. This is a good sign and indicates that you have beaten lots of lovely air into the mixture, which will make it all fluffy and perfect throughout.

ORANGE AND SAFFRON SAND CAKE

THIS CAKE IS buckets and spades, yellow light on closed eyelids and the smell of sun cream. Think of summer holidays, a skip along the sand and cherry flashes of bougainvillea.

SERVES 9

160g caster sugar
2 medium free-range
    eggs
100g ground almonds
200g fine-ground
    polenta
2 tsp baking powder
¼ tsp salt
a couple of generous
    pinches of saffron
    strands
zest of 2 small oranges
    (juicing varieties,
    such as Seville,
    are best)
200g topped, tailed,
    peeled and finely
    grated **carrot**

FOR THE SYRUP

freshly squeezed juice
    from 2 juicing
    oranges (300ml)
150g clear honey
small pinch of saffron
    strands

YOU WILL NEED

a 22cm-square x 5cm-
    deep brownie tin

1 Preheat the oven to 180°C/350°F/gas mark 4. Lightly grease the bottom and sides of the tin with either a bit of butter on its own paper, or else some vegetable oil and a pastry brush.

2 Beat the sugar with the eggs for 3 minutes until pale and fluffy. Add the ground almonds, polenta, baking powder, salt, saffron, orange zest and grated carrot, and mix until combined.

3 Pour the mixture into the tin. Cover the tin with foil and cook for **1 hour 15 minutes** on a rack near the bottom of the oven.

4 To make the syrup, put the orange juice into a saucepan and add the honey and saffron strands. Bring to the boil, then take off the heat. Let it stand for at least 10 minutes to infuse and give it a stir to combine everything. Set it aside until the cake is out of the oven.

5 Once cooked, run the thin blade of a knife around the sides of the cake to loosen. With the help of a skewer, prick the cake so that it ends up looking like a beach after a sand crab has been around. Finally, pour the syrup evenly over the surface and let it stand for 15 minutes in the tin.

6 Serve directly from the tin as the cake will be rather delicate and prone to crumbling. Mine is like this too and it's the sandcastle effect on the plate that I love so much.

TRUST ME TIPS

• Using sharp-flavoured oranges will really make a difference to the flavour of this cake.

• If freezing this cake, simply leave the syrup stage until the cake is completely defrosted, then proceed in the usual way.

CARROT CAKE

THIS CAKE IS the great-great-aunt of all the ones in this book. She has lived through several wars, and likes to read her newspaper in bed with lace gloves so that she doesn't stain her fingers with the ink.

SERVES 12

1 orange (juicing varieties, such as Seville, are best)
150g sultanas
80g pecans, roughly chopped
3 medium free-range eggs
160g light Muscovado sugar
280g scrubbed and finely grated **carrot**
150g white rice flour
80g ground almonds
2 tsp cinnamon
2 tsp baking powder
1 tsp vanilla extract
¼ tsp salt

FOR THE ICING

35g unsalted butter, cold and cubed
200g icing sugar
2 tsp freshly squeezed lime juice
35g cream cheese
finely grated zest of ½ lime

YOU WILL NEED

two 18cm-diameter x 5cm-deep loose-bottomed tins
a timer

1 Preheat the oven to 160°C/325°F/gas mark 3 and grease the bottom and sides of the tins. Cut two circles of baking parchment the same size as the base of the tins and use them to line the bases. Grease again.

2 Finely grate the zest of the orange on to a plate and set it aside, then squeeze the orange and soak the sultanas in the juice whilst you make up the rest of the recipe.

3 Toast the pecans in the oven whilst you get the rest of the ingredients ready. They shouldn't have time to burn, but set a timer for 10 minutes just in case.

4 Whisk the eggs and sugar for a full 5 minutes until pale coffee coloured. Add the grated carrot and orange zest before beating again briefly to incorporate.

5 Finally, mix the flour, ground almonds, cinnamon, baking powder, vanilla extract and salt together with the help of the whisk until all the ingredients are combined.

6 Add the sultanas, along with any orange juice left in the bowl, and the toasted pecans. Mix with a spatula until they are well dotted around.

7 Divide the mixture evenly between the two tins. Place them in the middle of the oven for **1 hour**.

8 Remove the cakes from the oven, unmould, turn out on to a wire rack and leave to cool completely, otherwise the icing will run off.

9 To make the cream-cheese icing, whisk the butter for a minute until light and softened. Next, add 100g of the icing sugar to the butter and whisk to a fine breadcrumb consistency. Add the lime juice and whisk again to a paste.

10 When you reach this stage, add the cream cheese and the zest of the lime, as well as the remaining icing sugar. Beat by hand with a wooden spoon to combine. Refrigerate for 15 minutes before icing the cold cake.

CONTINUED OVERLEAF

• I haven't found the need to sieve the icing sugar, but mine wasn't very lumpy. If you have slightly old icing sugar, however, it might well have dried out a little. If this is the case, simply sieve it before making the icing.

• If by misfortune the icing curdles and turns slightly grainy, simply adjust the mixture by adding more icing sugar until it is whole again.

Autumn Apple and Cider Cake

THIS CAKE IS DIGNIFIED. She takes her time but is never late, and hates shop-bought marmalade. She always remembers your birthday, and her presents are tied with real ribbon. Patient and wise, this cake is a warm shawl against the biting wind and the death of the year.

SERVES 12

1 medium cooking
    apple (roughly
    260g whole)
½ lemon
3 medium free-range
    eggs
180g caster sugar
150g white rice flour
150g ground almonds
2 tsp baking powder
1 tsp mixed spice
1 tsp ground ginger
¼ tsp salt
200g topped, tailed,
    peeled and super-
    finely grated
    parsnip
1 tsp vanilla extract
200ml dry cider

FOR THE TOP

1 smallish cooking apple
freshly squeezed juice of
    ½ lemon
icing sugar for dusting

YOU WILL NEED

a 23cm-diameter x
    7cm-deep loose-
    bottomed tin
kitchen string

1 Preheat the oven to 200°C/400°F/gas mark 6. Lightly brush the base and sides of the tin with a little vegetable oil.

2 Cut out two circles of baking parchment the same size as the base of the tin. Also cut one circle of the tin foil slightly larger than the diameter of the tin.

3 Take a sheet of baking parchment roughly 75cm long. Fold the long stretch of paper over itself three times. Snip along the folded edge at 2cm intervals; the cuts should also measure roughly 2cm. Line the sides of the tin with this paper, with the cut edge at the bottom, so that the little snipped bits fold into the centre of the tin. You may need to use your fingers to bend them into obedience.

4 Once all the little tags are facing the centre and the sides of the tin are all covered in thick paper, place the first circle of baking parchment on the base of the tin, then lightly brush it and the paper round the sides with a little oil. Finally, place the second circle of paper over the first, and brush this one with oil too. Set the lined tin aside until needed.

5 Peel, core and chop the medium apple into 1cm cubes. The size of the apple chunks is really important, so don't be tempted to cut them too big or the cake won't rise as well. Pop them into a small bowl and squeeze over them the juice of the half lemon with your hand; this will prevent them from turning brown and losing their firm texture. Give them a quick toss to make sure that they are all coated before setting aside.

6 Without coring, slice the small apple for the top as thinly as you can manage it through the middle, removing any pips. This is easiest to do with a serrated knife. There should be at least 4 thin slices with a pretty star shape in the centre. Run the remaining lemon juice over them on both sides, and make sure that they are well covered in the liquid. Set aside until needed.

CONTINUED OVERLEAF

7 In a large mixing bowl, whisk together the eggs and sugar until pale and tripled in volume (this takes roughly 3 minutes on 'full speed ahead').

8 Add the flour, ground almonds, baking powder, mixed spice, ginger, salt and grated parsnip, and give a thoroughly good mix. Pour both the vanilla extract and the cider over this mixture, and whizz briefly again to loosen it. Finally, fold in the apple cubes and tip the mixture into the prepared tin.

9 Place the apple slices on top of the cake and then place the foil circle over the tin, making sure that it is not touching the surface of the cake. Gently crinkle the foil over the edge of the tin to secure it. Tie a piece of string round the tin, over the foil, to make sure that the foil doesn't let in the sun and tan the cake in the hot oven.

10 Bake on a wire rack in the bottom of the oven for **2 hours**, without peeping. Once cooked, remove from the oven, take off the foil lid, and brush the apple slices on the top with a little water. Be careful not to wet the cake around the slices. Sieve a generous sprinkling of icing sugar over the lot.

11 Unmould and serve either cold with warm Crème Anglaise flavoured with 12 scratches of nutmeg (see pages 50–1), or warm with Crème à l'Armagnac (see page 20).

TRUST ME TIPS

• Organic ground ginger is much much more powerful than non-organic . . .

• The paper faff is crucial to prevent the cake from scorching. It needs both the protection of the paper and the overall heat of the oven at this high temperature to give it the rocket power to lift the apple contained within the cake.

• The foil sheet really needs to be on tightly, otherwise the air in the oven can lift it and the cake will certainly catch on top. The character of this cake is to be pale and patient, which is why it may take longer, but it will be *right*.

• This cake does not freeze well, and is best served warm or just cool.

Cake Diaries

CHOCOLATE AND PEANUT BUTTER CUPCAKES

Testing Number 1: 12 April

Not a bad first attempt and certainly extremely encouraging for a chocolate cupcake début! Pumpkin and peanut butter seem to be made for each other . . . I'm hoping for a bit more bounce, a slightly shinier crumb face and a more luxurious icing on my next testing. At the moment the balance of sweet/salt both in the icing and the cake has gone for a Burton and needs tweaking. Cheeky little blighters, these.

Testing Number 3: 13 April

Eureka! Seriously, this is an unhoped-for success story. This icing *defines* naughtiness . . . and who would have thought that boiling water was the answer! I love it.

ORANGE AND CARDAMOM STEAMED SPONGE

Testing Number 1: 1 October

I can definitely improve on this recipe as it stands . . .

Testing Number 2: 1 October

What an extraordinary difference those changes made. Amazing really when you consider they were only a couple of smallish ones. This is now a delicate, delightful, fragrant young girl – all blonde and September gold. The cardamom and orange balance is now gorgeous and well matched. I'm left wondering which syrup/custard would be a good companion? It may come to me later as I'm really tired this afternoon – puddings always do take it out of me.

CRÈME ANGLAISE

Testing Number 1: 16 September

Silk. Wonderful. I'm contented. This took for ever but is so worth it. It reminds me of love.

STEAMED GOLDEN SYRUP SPONGE PUDDING

Testing Number 1: 15 September

Halfway through cooking I thought, 'Oh God, disaster!' I didn't have a real pudding basin so was using a Pyrex bowl instead, and had forgotten to secure a proper lid with paper and string. This means that the cooking time won't be represented properly . . .

Testing Number 2: 16 September

Right, I've done it properly this time. I'm going to give it an hour to start with. High, high hopes, my dear. And who would have thought that turnip had such a manly combination of strength and feather? It needs to go down by 50g but otherwise it's perfect.

MISS MARPLE SEED CAKE

Testing Number 1: 16 September

It's gone into the tin feeling too loose and too sweet. I may have to address the situation with either ground almonds, potato or flour – or a combination of all three. I hope that the brandy flavour wafts through . . .

Testing Number 3: 16 September

Well, it doesn't taste of brandy but in every other respect this cake is ready to live! What fun today has been!

ORANGE AND SAFFRON SAND CAKE

Testing Number 4: 23 September

I haven't seen this old friend since 3 June – she nearly hit the graveyard then, but I'm not quite ready to give up on her yet. New tactics are afoot in my camp. I have re-read Cake Diary 1 and amended a few things: firstly I will up the polenta to 200g (in search of sand), then add some orange juice (to help make the sand wet). I'm changing the tin (to help her breathe) and also upping the honey in the syrup . . . The best attempt so far but not perfect yet. She's still a bit bitter and unhappy.

Testing Number 5: 23 September

Tried again with more almonds too. When the cake cools down, she tightens and I don't like it. Why won't the grains separate more? Maybe I will take the oranges down to two instead of three. This might also solve the bitterness, come to think of it. The boiling of the oranges is a terrible palaver . . . Let's go again. Not far off. Take heart, H.

Testing Number 6: 25 September

This is now starting to feel like an epic! It's so frustrating because I *know* this cake already and she is so lovely: all golden sand and light and holidays . . . In my daydream I just had a brainwave! I'll replace the swede with carrot that has wood rather than gum for a backbone. Let's go for it!

Testing Number 7: 25 September

I'm so close I could almost touch her . . . but then she goes all tight and frightened when she cools down. This is terribly upsetting as I don't understand what she wants. On a positive note, the carrot is miles and miles of beach better than swede. It has lightened her up a lot and helped her to lift upwards. I'm not going to look at this recipe for a while because she's starting to make me sad. Maybe the answer will come if I don't look too hard.

Testing Number 8: 14 December

Something magical has just happened: I had all my ingredients out for another go at hunting for sand, and I made the cake without really concentrating. In my distraction, I completely forgot to boil the oranges and simply grated them into the mixture instead. I could have thrown myself out of the window I was so cross with myself! I nearly chucked the cake mixture in the bin altogether, but didn't, as I thought at least I could feed it to the birds . . . When I took it out of the oven and cut into it, I couldn't believe my eyes: SAND! Beautiful light, hopeful sand! Exactly the texture I have been looking for these last six months. *Finalmente*. Sand. Thank you. I am thrilled.

CHRISTMAS
CUPCAKES

CHRISTMAS CUPCAKES

THESE CUPCAKES ARE a group of irrepressible cousins, scuttling down the corridor . . . They always spend Christmas together and know the drill: they'll raid the dressing-up box and put on a play.

MAKES 12

80g sultanas or raisins
120g candied peel
4 tbsp brandy
4 medium free-range eggs
100g dark Muscovado
    sugar
¼ tsp salt
200g topped, tailed,
    peeled and very
    finely grated **carrot**
very finely grated zest of
    2 unwaxed lemons
100g white rice flour
50g ground almonds
2 tsp baking powder
2 tsp ground ginger
1 tsp mixed spice
15 scratches of grated
    nutmeg
1 tsp ground cinnamon
60g glacé cherries, halved
60g pecans, roughly
    chopped

FOR THE ICING
1 quantity Snow
    Meringue Icing (see
    page 85), replacing
    1 tbsp water with 1
    tbsp brandy for a bit
    of extra buzz

YOU WILL NEED
a 12-hole muffin tray
12 cupcake cases (see
    page xxvii for exact
    size)

1 Preheat the oven to 180°C/350°F/gas mark 4 and line the muffin tray with the paper cases.

2 Soak the sultanas and candied peel in a bowl with the brandy before you start on the rest of the recipe.

3 Whisk the eggs, sugar and salt in a large mixing bowl for 3 full minutes until light coffee coloured and fluffy. Add the grated carrot and lemon zest and whisk until combined.

4 Fold in the flour, ground almonds, baking powder, ginger, mixed spice, nutmeg and cinnamon, along with the glacé cherries and pecans, with a large metal spoon until they are all mixed together and singing from the same carol sheet. Finally, add the soaked sultanas, candied peel and brandy, and mix in with the metal spoon.

5 Spoon the mixture carefully into the cases, making sure that they are roughly even and that the mixture comes four fifths of the way up the sides. Place in the middle of the oven for **30 minutes**. Now is the time to make the Snow Meringue Icing (see page 85).

6 Once the cupcakes are out of the oven, take them out of the tin and sit them on a wire rack for 10 minutes to cool. Ice them individually and serve, or keep un-iced in a tin until needed. Store for up to 3 days in an airtight container.

TRUST ME TIPS

• It is even more important here than in some of the other recipes to grate the carrot very, very finely. This cake mixture wants to be smooth and light in order to cushion so many boisterous chunks of fruit and nut.

BEETROOT CHOCOLATE FUDGE

THIS FUDGE IS A LOVEABLE BOY of about nine, who won't be pushed or made to walk any faster than feels right to him. Patience is required but it's completely worth the effort. You may find that he grows on you – a bit like Schubert does.

SERVES 25

200g peeled and cubed
    raw **beetroot**
450g caster sugar
30g unsalted butter
335g condensed milk
½ tsp salt
200g dark chocolate
    (70% cocoa solids
    essential), broken
    into squares

YOU WILL NEED

a 22cm-square x 5cm-
    deep brownie tin
a blender
a heatproof spatula
a timer

1 Cover the base of the tin with baking parchment and grease the parchment lightly.

2 Place the grated beetroot in a medium-sized saucepan with enough water to cover it. Boil the beetroot for 8 minutes until it is totally cooked through. Discard the water before whizzing thoroughly to a purée. This purée needs to be very fine so that the fudge is not lumpy, so please be pedantic over this point.

3 Put all the ingredients except the chocolate into a medium non-stick saucepan over a low heat and stir with the spatula to combine, so that the condensed milk and sugar are well introduced to one another and the butter starts to melt.

4 Warm gently on the lowest possible heat until the sugar has completely dissolved and there are no gritty sand grains at the bottom or on the sides of the pan at all. This will take 15 minutes. It's a good idea to stir at 2-minute intervals here, just to make sure that the butter is melting and that everyone is making friends. This stage is crucial to the success of the recipe and must be given the time it needs to get there, so please be patient if you want to avoid Grumpy Fudge.

5 Once all the sugar grains have dissolved, add the chocolate chunks and let them dissolve slowly for 1 minute. Only when there is a peaceful pool of dark liquid in the saucepan is it safe to turn up the heat a fraction (and I really do mean the most minute amount – say, one notch on your setting) and get ready to stir gently for the next 15 minutes exactly.

6 Make sure that you move your spatula over the entire base of the pan as well as into the corners in a patient but thorough motion. You can expect to hear a slight sizzle or 'zipping' noise, which is where the sugar mixture has marginally overheated – this is perfectly healthy. If, on the other hand, you hear hissing sounds, it's likely that the temperature is too high. Don't waste time feeling embarrassed by your impatient behaviour, simply turn down the heat and sing to the mixture to soothe it. You'll know it's calm again when the odd large bubble starts popping on the surface.

7 Once the fudge has had its full time, remove it from the heat and beat it by hand for 3 minutes exactly, which will thicken the fudge and start to set it. If you find that it is becoming too heavy before the whole 3 minutes are up, stop beating – this means that it is ready.

8 Pour the fudge carefully into the prepared tin. It will be setting very fast at this stage, so it's a good idea to have a palette knife to hand to help the spatula with its workload. Stroke the surface of the fudge over with the rubber end of the spatula to smooth the top. Set it aside for at least half an hour to cool.

9 Cut into squares and serve, or store in an airtight container for up to 2 weeks.

TRUST ME TIPS

• The correct spatula is rather important in this recipe – and by that I mean one that is flexible and doesn't keep on losing its head in the mixture (if you get my drift) but is able to remain sanguine, reliable and attached throughout.

• I feel I ought to warn you that you will spend an Olympian amount of energy, first stirring, then beating this fudge. It's up to you, but I normally take off my jumper and tune into the radio before starting the recipe, ready for the workout. If you have a small trouble that you want to think through, or if you are particularly cross, this part of the recipe doubles as therapy.

PLUM PUDDING

I DON'T LIKE CHRISTMAS PUDDING. Its ominous countenance makes me sit up straight and mind my manners when it's brought in. Instead, the ingredients in this pudding are mellowed by a touch of Jamaican Calypso music and a dose of rum. This pudding is lighter, swings her hips when she walks, but still provokes the tingle of Christmas in the air.

SERVES 12

150g plump and juicy
    raisins
100g currants
100g mixed candied
    peel
125ml rum
3 medium free-range eggs
100g dark Muscovado
    sugar
150g ripe banana
200g topped, tailed,
    peeled and finely
    grated **parsnip**
finely grated zest of 2
    unwaxed lemons
100g white rice flour
100g ground almonds
2 tsp baking powder
¼ tsp salt
2 tbsp mixed spice
1 tsp nutmeg
1 tbsp ginger
2 tsp cinnamon

FOR THE TOP

100ml rum, a match and
    a sprig of holly

YOU WILL NEED

a really big saucepan
    (a stock pan is ideal)
a 2-litre pudding basin
kitchen string

1 Put a full kettle of water on to boil and lightly grease the base and sides of the pudding bowl.

2 Take a sheet of tin foil (about 30cm square) and another of baking parchment the same size. Place these sheets on top of each other with the parchment on the bottom. Make a pleat about 6cm wide in the middle of both layers, so that the two are pleated together and the steam can billow up into the pleat. This will end up looking like a milkmaid's hat once it's safely on the pudding.

3 Grease the parchment side of this lid (the one which will be in contact with the surface of the pudding) and set aside for later.

4 Take another length of foil, about 70cm long, and fold it over and over to make a strong strip roughly 8cm wide.

5 Cover the raisins, currants and candied peel with the rum and place in a bowl under a layer of cling film. Set aside to soak.

6 Whisk the eggs and sugar for no less than 5 minutes with a hand-held whisk, until tripled in volume and cappuccino coloured; the mixture should hold a ribbon trail when you lift up the beaters. Mash the banana with a fork and add to the fluffy mixture with the grated parsnip and lemon zest. Beat to incorporate.

7 Now add the flour, ground almonds, baking powder, salt, mixed spice, nutmeg, ginger and cinnamon. Beat this for a minute with an electric whisk until well mixed in. Finally, add the soaked fruit and peel, as well as the rum, to the mixing bowl and combine with a wooden spoon until well mixed.

8 Pour the contents into the prepared basin and cover with the foil-and-parchment lid, foil side up. Wind the string twice round the lip of the basin, making sure that you leave no gaps where water could get through. Tie the string firmly with a knot to secure the lid.

CONTINUED OVERLEAF

9 Trim the parchment and foil layers carefully so that only a couple of centimetres are left below the string line. Any more and the water will catch and ride up inside the lid; any less and the steam inside the pudding will push the lid upwards and let the water in.

10 Lower the basin into the saucepan with the help of the folded length of foil and pour boiling water from the kettle into the pan until it reaches the lip of the basin. Make sure that the water level comes up to the lip but not over it, as this might force a small amount of water into the pudding mixture.

11 Boil for **4 hours 30 minutes** on a steady low boil (as opposed to a frantic, spluttering one) with the lid on the pan, making sure to top up the level of water so that it never goes below the lip (roughly every 30 minutes).

12 Remove the pudding with the help of the foil strip. Tip it out of its basin on to your serving plate and leave it to sit in steaming glory whilst you warm the rum. This is the time to place the holly sprig if you have one.

13 Heat the rum in a small saucepan for a couple of minutes until really warm but by no means boiling. Very carefully strike a match to light the liquid and pour the flaming drink over the pudding. Serve immediately and with the lights dimmed right down.

TRUST ME TIPS

• It is absolutely vital to make sure that no water *whatsoever* boils into the pudding mixture or it will turn it to heavy, sodden mush. In order to protect the pudding from a watery end, you should carefully observe the advice in the recipe about fitting and securing the foil-and-parchment lid.

• If you boil the rum that is going over the pudding at the end, all the alcoholic content will be boiled off and it will not light.

• I was thrilled to discover that I could not only cook this pudding a few days in advance, freeze it and then warm it through in its basin in hot water all over again – but that I could also microwave it! I know that the m-word is pretty nasty when associated with cake, but this is a good time to make use of it. Make sure that you microwave the defrosted pudding on low for about 10 minutes (as opposed to high for 5 minutes).

BEACH AND BLANKET
FRUIT CAKE For Freddie Wyvill

THERE IS A PATIENT BEACH at the edge of the world called Luskintyre. She stretches her long white legs for miles. This cake belongs there amid the pale dunes, with a blanket, coffee in a Thermos flask and rosy faces, full of winter wind and sea spray.

SERVES 12

150g sultanas
120g glacé cherries
    (I prefer the dark
    red ones, but it's up
    to you)
100g whole almonds,
    blanched
1 tsp almond essence
3 medium free-range
    eggs
150g light Muscovado
    sugar
250g peeled and grated
    butternut squash
finely grated zest of
    1 orange
finely grated zest of ½
    unwaxed lemon
150g white rice flour
100g ground almonds
2 tsp baking powder
¼ tsp salt
a little golden caster
    sugar

YOU WILL NEED
a 23cm-diameter x
    7cm-deep loose-
    bottomed tin

1 Preheat the oven to 160°C/325°F/gas mark 3. Line the base of the tin with baking parchment and brush a little vegetable oil over the parchment and the naked sides of the tin.

2 Put the sultanas, glacé cherries and blanched almonds on a plate. Pour the almond essence over them and set aside.

3 Whisk the eggs and sugar in a large mixing bowl for 4 minutes until they have tripled in volume and look suitably light and full of air and life. Add the grated butternut squash, and orange and lemon zest, and whisk until fully combined.

4 Next, add the flour, ground almonds, baking powder and salt. Finally, fold in the fruit, nuts and almond essence with the help of a metal spoon.

5 Pour the mixture into the tin and bake in the bottom of the oven for **1 hour**.

6 Once cooked, remove from the oven and sprinkle with caster sugar. Leave to cool in the tin for 10 minutes. Run a thin-bladed knife around the edge and unmould carefully on to a wire rack. Eat straight away or store in an airtight container for up to 4 days.

MULLED WHITE WINE JELLIES

THE MAGIC OF JELLY is Suspension. Like a helium balloon, or a cloud in the sky, it's beautifully illogical that they can hang inside invisible jelly . . .

MAKES 12 JELLIES

750ml white wine
500ml dessert wine,
    such as Moscatel
1½ litres water
3 sticks of cinnamon
5 star anise
10 cardamom pods
4 bay leaves
50g piece raw ginger,
    peeled and finely
    sliced
300g caster sugar
1 vanilla pod, split
    lengthways
3 strips of orange zest
16 leaves of gelatine

TO DECORATE
redcurrants or star anise,
    baby bay leaves from
    the mixture, etc.

**FOR 'HIGH DAYS
AND HOLIDAYS'
DECORATION**
flecks of gold leaf

YOU WILL NEED
pretty, clear glasses or
    individual glass bowls
tweezers or a wooden
    skewer

1 Set out twelve glasses or small individual glass bowls.

2 Place all the ingredients except the gelatine into a large saucepan and heat gently. Do not bring to boiling point, but do coax the liquid into a state of heat haze, which happens just before the simmering point is reached. Once you are there, maintain this temperature inside the pan for 20 minutes. Stir occasionally to check that the sugar has dissolved.

3 Take the pan off the heat. Pour the liquid through a sieve into a large non-metal mixing bowl and cool for 15 minutes. Keep the used spices for decorating the jellies later on.

4 When the 15 minutes are up and once the mulled wine is the temperature of blood, turn your attention to the gelatine stage of the recipe. Put the gelatine leaves in a small mixing bowl, cover with cold water and let them sit for 2 minutes, until softened. Wring them out thoroughly in your hands before dropping them into the mulled wine. Stir for 2 minutes to dissolve completely.

5 Ladle the mixture into the glasses and place them in the fridge. Set a timer for 4–5 hours (depending on how cold and full your fridge is), after which they will have set, even if still only a 'soft set'.

6 Next, use a clean pair of tweezers or a wooden skewer to place your chosen garnish into each glass halfway up and hold it there for a couple of seconds to secure it. It is a lot easier to suspend things nearer the edges than in the middle of any jelly. Once the garnish is suspended in the jelly, leave them to chill until you are ready to serve them.

TRUST ME TIPS

• If the mulled wine mixture isn't hot enough to dissolve the gelatine completely, simply heat up a mug's worth of water until hot (but by no means scalding) and dissolve the gelatine in that before adding it to the mulled wine.

76

CONTINUED OVERLEAF

- The reason that these take at least 4 hours to set is that I have used the minimum amount of gelatine possible, in order to have delicate jellies rather than tennis balls.

- The setting time will vary hugely, depending on how cold your fridge is (which in turn will depend on how full it is). Jelly is notoriously fickle.

- Testing for 'setness' is easy. Simply prod the surface of the liquid gently with the tip of your finger. If it has started to set, a small fingerprint will be left behind.

- It is important to use a light white wine, such as Pinot Grigio; avoid Chardonnay or other heavily oaked wines. I hate to be a party-pooper, but I'm afraid that, despite the spices, using up really horrid wine won't make for a pleasant and delicate jelly in the long run.

- If you can't be bothered with the hassle of making jelly, this recipe is completely delicious as plain Mulled White Wine. Simply stop the recipe after the initial 20-minute heat haze for a warm mug of delicately spiced party fun.

- I think it a real shame to serve these jellies in anything other than glass (especially if you have suspended twinkling star anise and gold leaf), as looking through the aquarium at the world inside is the fun of it. You can find gold leaf in most specialist cake shops.

- After all this palaver, the really wonderful thing to remember about jelly is that it is the ultimate dessert to make in advance – up to 4 days if you want to – and nothing will go wrong once it's made. Isn't that a lovely thought?

PECORINO AND CHIVE SCONES WITH WALNUTS

THERE IS SOMETHING SO HELPFUL about scones – and tidy. They satisfy homely urges of warm kitchen smells, and board games when it's raining out. When the news everywhere is red with panic, you can rely on these inquisitive little troopers to make you feel useful.

MAKES 10–12

250g white spelt flour, plus a little extra for rolling

40g pecorino, finely grated, plus extra for the top

2 tsp baking powder

½ tsp bicarbonate of soda

¼ tsp salt (optional)

a couple of grinds of black pepper

1 tbsp clear honey

220g topped, tailed and finely grated **courgette**

40g walnuts, roughly chopped

3 tbsp/small bunch of chives, finely snipped

a little milk or egg yolk

YOU WILL NEED

a 6cm pastry-cutter

a food processor

1 Preheat the oven to 200°C/400°F/gas mark 6 and line a baking sheet with foil and baking parchment. Lightly brush the parchment with a little vegetable oil.

2 Put the flour, pecorino, baking powder, bicarbonate of soda, salt (if using) and black pepper into the bowl of the food processor, followed by the honey and grated courgette. Pulse until almost fully combined, then add the walnuts and chives. Run your knife around the edges, then pulse again until a sticky dough is formed. It doesn't have to be in one piece, just as long as the elements of wet and dry have come together.

3 Tip the dough out on to a lightly floured surface and bring together with gentle care, not putting too much pressure on the dough, as it is sensitive to stress. Lightly roll out to 4cm thick, before cutting out your circles. With all scones, it is advisable not to twist the cutter, as this brings them up wonky in the oven. A firm and confident slice downwards is all that is needed for well-brought-up scones.

4 Lightly brush each scone with a tiny bit of milk or egg yolk, and sprinkle a generous pinch of grated pecorino over each one.

5 Place in the top of the oven for **17 minutes**, at which point they should be golden and well risen. These are excellent served with vegetable soup. Fill them with mild goat's cheese and sweet caramelized red onions.

TREACLE STEAMED SPONGE

THIS IS THE PERSON you want to be sitting next to at dinner. 'Treacle' nearly sounds like 'twinkle', which is exactly what is sitting in the corner of his eye . . .

SERVES 10

3 medium free-range
    eggs
200g dark Muscovado
    sugar
250g topped, tailed,
    peeled and finely
    grated **carrot**
finely grated zest of
    1 small orange
    (juicing varieties,
    such as Seville,
    are best)
2 tbsp treacle
150g white rice flour
100g ground almonds
2 tsp baking powder
¼ tsp salt
2 tsp ground ginger

FOR THE BASE

30g pecans, roughly
    chopped
2 tbsp golden syrup

YOU WILL NEED

a really big saucepan
    (a stock pan is ideal)
a 2-litre pudding basin
kitchen string

1 Put a full kettle of water on to boil.

2 Take a long (say 70cm) length of tin foil. Fold it over and over itself in a 6cm strip. This will be used to lower the pudding basin in and out of the boiling water later on.

3 Lightly grease the sides and base of the pudding basin. Measure out a length of baking parchment (about 30cm square). Cut a piece of foil of the same size and lay it on top of the sheet of parchment. Make a pleat about 6cm wide in the middle of both layers, so that the two are pleated together and the steam can billow up into the pleat.

4 Grease the parchment side of this lid (which will be in contact with the surface of the pudding) and set aside until needed.

5 Pour the pecans and golden syrup into the bowl of the pudding basin. You will find it easier to spoon the syrup from the tin if you run your spoon under boiling water first.

6 Whisk the eggs with the sugar for a full 5 minutes, until fluffy and cappuccino coloured. The mixture should hold a trail when you remove the beaters. Add the grated carrot, orange zest and treacle to the mixing bowl. Again, it is useful to run the measuring spoon under boiling water before plunging it into the treacle, as this helps to loosen it. Whisk to combine for a minute.

7 Finally, add the flour, ground almonds, baking powder, salt and ginger, then beat until all the ingredients are fully introduced to one another.

8 Pour the pudding mixture into the basin and cover with the parchment-and-foil lid, with the foil side uppermost. Wrap the string twice around the basin, making sure that you leave no gaps where water could get through. Tie the string firmly with a knot to secure the lid.

9 Trim the parchment and foil layers carefully so that only a couple of centimetres are left below the string line. Any more and the water will catch and ride up inside the lid; any less and the steam inside the pudding will push the lid upwards and let the water in.

10 Place the basin squarely on the foil strip and lower the pudding into the saucepan. Pour boiling water from the kettle into the pan so that it comes up to the lip of the basin.

11 Put the lid on the pan (to avoid too much water evaporating), making sure that the ends of the foil strip stick out over the pan sides. Boil on medium water roll for **1 hour 30 minutes**.

12 Remove the pudding from the pan using the folded strip of foil and leave to cool for 20 minutes. This would be perfect served with Crème Anglaise (see pages 50–1), with ¼ tsp ground ginger added to the milk at the beginning of the recipe.

Banana and Toffee Sticky Cake

TOFFEE IS A BIT OF A RASCAL, and delights in making a mess and then running to hide. Luckily, banana is unfazed and copes with this tricky behaviour in its usual horizontal style. This is not a household with much shouting, although plenty of squealing and peals of laughter seem to ring around the staircase and echo in the bathroom.

SERVES 9

3 medium free-range
     eggs
160g light Muscovado
     sugar
250g peeled and finely
     grated **butternut
     squash**
1 tbsp vanilla extract
50g white rice flour
100g ground almonds
2 tsp baking powder
¼ tsp salt
80g brazil nuts, roughly
     chopped (or
     use pecans or
     macadamias)
150g banana, peeled and
     finely sliced

FOR THE SYRUP
50g unsalted butter
100g golden syrup
3 tbsp boiling water

YOU WILL NEED
a 22cm-square x 5cm-
     deep brownie tin
a timer

1 Preheat the oven to 180°C/350°F/gas mark 4. Line the base of the tin with baking parchment. Grease the parchment and the sides of the tin with a little butter.

2 In a large mixing bowl, whisk the eggs and sugar until pale and cappuccino coloured (roughly 5 minutes on full blast). Beat in the grated butternut squash and vanilla extract with the whisk until well combined.

3 Whisk in the flour, ground almonds, baking powder and salt until smooth. Finally, with the help of a spatula, mix in the brazil nuts and banana (reserve a small handful of banana slices for the top).

4 Tip the mixture into the prepared tin. Dot the reserved banana slices over the top of the cake (flat, so that they look like circles) before placing the cake in the oven for **35 minutes**.

5 Once cooked, remove the cake from the oven and let it stand to cool in its tin while you make the toffee syrup.

6 In a medium-sized saucepan, melt the butter and the golden syrup with the water on a low heat until the butter has become liquid. Turn up the heat and, once boiling point has been reached (when the surface is covered in smallish bubbles), continue to boil hard for 3 minutes exactly. For anyone who is unsure about making toffee or hasn't done it before, I have included a foolproof step-by-step explanation overleaf.

7 Once the 3 minutes are up, take the pan off the heat immediately and beat the bubbles out of the mixture, which should take no longer than 30 seconds.

8 Drizzle the hot liquid over the cake quickly, which couldn't be happier for the warm, sticky syrup. I tend to tilt the cake in its tin left, right, back and forth whilst the toffee is still hot and runny to get

CONTINUED OVERLEAF

it spread over the surface. If you go and answer the telephone even for 10 seconds, you will have missed the boat and the toffee will refuse to move, let alone run. If this happens, I'm afraid that the only thing to do is start the toffee stage again and curse yourself for thinking that you could outwit the stuff.

9 Once the toffee has drenched the top of the cake, let it stand to sink in for 10 minutes before serving. This is heaven with vanilla or toffee ice cream, or Crème au Rhum (page 20).

TRUST ME TIPS

• The cooked cake will come out of the oven looking a bit like an Aero chocolate bar on the surface and will be very springy to the touch. This is totally normal and no cause for concern.

STEP-BY-STEP GUIDE TO MAKING TOFFEE SAUCE IN 3 MINUTES

Taming toffee requires confidence. Dissolve the butter with the other ingredients on a medium heat, then turn the heat up to reach full boil. Start the timer for 3 minutes. Each stage lasts roughly one minute and you can expect the progression in the pan to go as follows:

1 The first stage of boiling will provide you with an angry mixture, made up of lots of little see-through bubbles that rise quickly to the surface of the liquid. They will huff and puff out their chests and get bigger. They will want to creep up the sides of the pan and escape, but won't succeed in a medium-sized pan. My pan is only 9cm deep and my toffee hasn't bubbled over yet.

2 At the second stage, you can expect slightly smaller (medium-sized) bubbles that don't come so far up the pan and are less angry than before. They will gradually accept defeat and retreat down the sides. The colour will start to turn from butter yellow to golden caramel.

3 The final stage is gloss and gloop. Although the bubbles have pride, and will therefore still be simmering with rebellious defiance at the bottom of the pan, they are not on the attack any more. The smell in the kitchen will be completely of melted butter.

4 When your timer bleeps to signal that 3 minutes are up, take the pan off the heat *immediately*. Whisk the bubbly mixture vigorously with a balloon whisk until the bubbles have completely disappeared and the battle is over.

Snow Meringue Icing

I HOPE THAT YOUR WHISK is in good physical shape, because this recipe will certainly give it a workout – think the north face of the Eiger.

**MAKES ENOUGH
TO ICE 12
CUPCAKES OR 1
WHOLE CAKE**

170g icing sugar
2 tbsp water
¼ tsp cream of tartar
white of 1 medium
    free-range egg
small pinch of salt

YOU WILL NEED
a hand-held electric
    whisk
a timer

1 Place all the ingredients in a big mixing bowl over a pan of boiling water. Stir with a clean metal spoon for 2 minutes exactly to dissolve the sugar.

2 When the mixture is warm and the 2 minutes are up, remove the bowl from the heat and beat with a hand-held electric whisk. Whisk for 9 minutes until cool. The mixture is ready to use when it's standing up like snow-covered Swiss peaks.

3 If piping the icing, simply fill your piping bag in the usual way. Be sure to ice the cakes (or cake) very quickly, as the icing will start to set and alter its flexibility as it sits – it likes to be used when just made.

TRUST ME TIPS

• Beating for longer than suggested will simply mean that the icing gets harder (the very end of the road being Royal icing, which is ideal if you fancy sacrificing a tooth on the altar of Traditional Wedding Cake). Timings are important here, I'm afraid, which is why I urge you to bring out the Kitchen Tyrant: a timer.

• This recipe is plain – by which I mean that it is as pure as the driven snow – but flavourings such as vanilla, rose water or brandy can be added, depending on the recipe the icing is accompanying. If adding a liquid flavouring, simply replace some or all of the 2 tbsp of water with the flavour of your choice, or, in the case of vanilla pods, split lengthways, scrape out the seeds and add them to the ingredients at the beginning of the recipe.

ALMOND HONEY CAKE WITH APRICOTS AND VANILLA

WHEN IT'S SUNNY, this cake prefers to teach arithmetic under the apple tree outside, which is why all the children in the classroom love her.

SERVES 10

1 vanilla pod, split
    lengthways
100g dried apricots
2 medium free-range eggs
180g clear honey (light-
    flavoured is best)
150g peeled and finely
    grated **sweet
    potato**
finely grated zest of ½
    unwaxed lemon
100g white rice flour
100g ground almonds
2 tsp baking powder
¼ tsp salt
100g whole blanched
    almonds (hold back
    12 or 15 almonds
    for the top)

FOR THE TOP

3 tbsp apricot jam,
    warmed in a pan
    and sieved, or 1 tbsp
    clear honey

YOU WILL NEED

a 23cm-diameter x
    7cm-deep loose-
    bottomed tin

1 Preheat the oven to 180°C/350°F/gas mark 4. Lightly grease the bottom and sides of the tin and line the base with a circle of baking parchment. Grease over this lightly once again.

2 Scrape out the seeds of the vanilla pod into a large mixing bowl and keep the empty pod.

3 Chop the apricots finely into small cubes (roughly half a centimetre is good). Soak them with the empty vanilla pod in just enough boiling water to cover them, in a small bowl covered with cling film.

4 Beat the eggs and honey in the mixing bowl with the vanilla seeds for 3 minutes. Add the grated sweet potato and lemon zest, and beat again until thoroughly well mixed. Add the flour, ground almonds, baking powder and salt, and mix until everything is well incorporated.

5 Drain the apricots thoroughly and discard the vanilla pod. Add the fruit to the mixing bowl along with the blanched almonds, mixing them in with a spatula (so that you don't break them up too much).

6 Tip the mixture into the prepared tin. Position the remaining almonds on the top of the cake in a pretty pattern before placing the cake in the middle of the oven for **45 minutes**.

7 Remove the cake from the oven and while it is still hot and in its tin, brush the apricot jam or honey over it with a pastry brush. Serve it on its own at teatime, or warm with vanilla ice cream for pudding.

TRUST ME TIPS

• Chop up the apricots small, as it makes a big difference to the overall result of the cake and really helps the rise.

• The glaze over the top is a bit faffy and old school, I admit. I prefer the jam because I like its slightly sharp tang and think that a bit of lip gloss over this cake is quite a pretty way to finish it off.

Cake Diaries

PLUM PUDDING

Testing Number 1: 5 November

It's not quite right but I have a strong idea of where to go from here. Thank goodness it doesn't resemble those dark and frightening-looking austere puddings that don't fit their name tag.

Testing Number 2: 5 November

My second attempt is miles better than the first but being the pedant that I am, I feel it could use just a tiny bit more spice and squidge. Up the ginger, mixed spice and banana, I think. These are aesthetic changes of character because the frame is wonderfully 'pudding'
as it is. What a terrific word 'pudding' is.

Testing Number 4: 6 November

I did it one last time to check the timings. She's ready to go out and sing.

BEACH AND BLANKET FRUIT CAKE FORMERLY KNOWN AS DUNDEE CAKE

Testing Number 1: 5 November

Hoppity skippity – a hole in one! He's magnificent. I love him. Just the right balance of moisture, strength, sweetness and citrus sharp. He's such a handsome size, such a happy colour. I'm going to change his name as he's too young and gentle for solid old Dundee Cake. This one is marriage material . . .

MULLED WHITE WINE JELLIES

Testing Number 1: 30 October

I thought initially that this one might have to hit the graveyard and then I had an idea . . . The problem was that it wasn't clear, it hadn't set and it tasted too strongly of raw booze. Number two and number three should be a cinch to solve but I was stuck on one until I thought of using white wine instead of red. This should work and look so, so pretty. I'll try again on Monday.

Testing Number 2: 4 November

I'm feeling murderous towards these as they obstinately refuse to set. I'm having no luck with them at all. I cannot understand how ten sheets of gelatine haven't glued the mixture to the spot! I will try to face it later on this week when I'm feeling strong again.

Testing Number 6: 16 December

Well, I didn't see this one becoming a six-part saga when I started out! I think that modern gelatine has changed. I have finally got a lovely texture that is set but not rubber, as well as a great Christmas flavour. I was fuming but they looked so pretty I couldn't be cross for long.

PECORINO AND CHIVE SCONES WITH WALNUTS

Testing Number 1: 30 September

Not bad at all – I would say a valiant and helpful effort on their parts (I always think of scones as being polite and helpful somehow). Thank you for your help with the washing up. I'm going to do it again with 30g less courgette to make them less 'poggy', as Granny describes it. The chive/cheese/walnut flavour (oh, and honey and black pepper) is lovely and no one is trying to boast louder than anybody else.

Testing Number 2: 30 September

We're there: a smile-making result. I feel useful again.

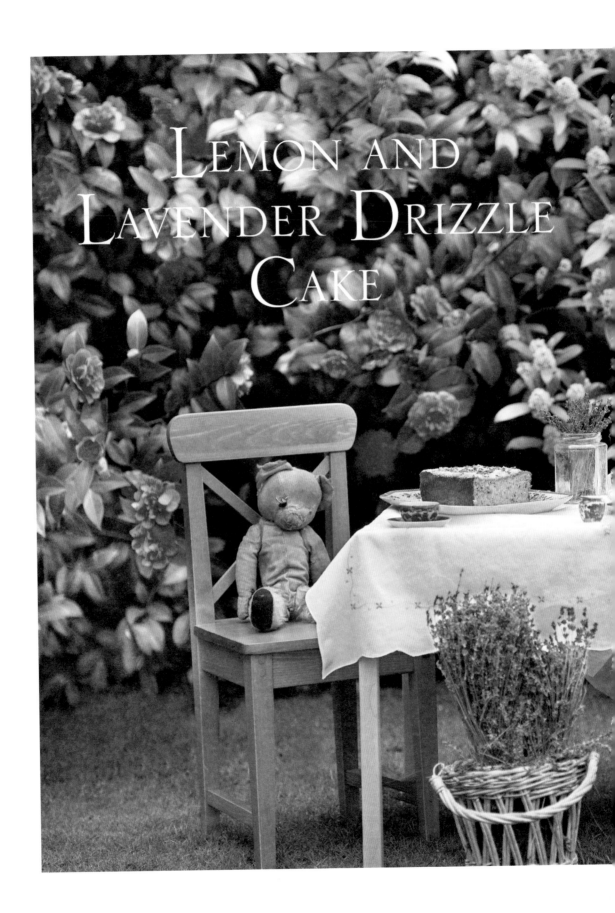

Lemon and Lavender Drizzle Cake

Lemon and Lavender Drizzle Cake

LEMON AND LAVENDER might be the flavours of Provence, but this is an English summer garden with the tinkling of china cups and saucers, the creaking of wicker furniture, and hats like straw mushrooms (pretending it's still 1912).

SERVES 8

200g swede, peeled and
    diced into 2cm cubes
120g clear honey
2 medium free-range eggs
finely grated zest of
    1 unwaxed lemon
1 heaped tbsp dried
    lavender flowers
60g white rice flour
60g ground almonds
2 tsp baking powder
¼ tsp salt

FOR THE DRIZZLE

3 tbsp golden granulated
    sugar
2 tbsp water
freshly squeezed juice
    of 1 lemon (100ml)

FOR THE TOP

1 tbsp golden granulated
    sugar
a few lavender flowers

YOU WILL NEED

a 19cm x 12cm x 8cm
    (1.7 litre) loaf tin
a microwave
a blender
a wooden skewer

1 Preheat the oven to 180°C/350°F/gas mark 4. Line the base of the tin with baking parchment and lightly brush the parchment and the sides of the tin with a little vegetable oil, then set aside.

2 Place the diced swede in a heatproof bowl with a splash of water and cover with cling film. Cook in the microwave on high for 7 minutes, until soft to the touch. Once cooked through, drain off the excess water and blend to a fine purée.

3 In a large mixing bowl, whisk the honey and eggs for 2 minutes, until bubbly.

4 Add the lemon zest, lavender flowers, flour, ground almonds, baking powder and salt, and whisk again for 20 seconds. Once all the ingredients are fully incorporated, whisk in the swede purée to combine.

5 Pour the mixture into the prepared tin and put in the middle of the oven for **30 minutes**.

6 Whilst the cake is cooking, prepare the drizzle. Dissolve the sugar in the water by heating slowly in a small pan. As soon as the sugar has dissolved, take off the heat and set aside. Add the lemon juice when the sugar syrup is cool.

7 Remove the cake from the oven, leave it in the tin and prick it right through to the bottom with a skewer so that it is covered in little holes. Drizzle the sweet lemon liquid over the cake. Do this while the cake is still hot and at its most absorbent. Finish off by sprinkling with the remaining sugar and the odd lavender flower before serving.

CONTINUED OVERLEAF

• Something about heating lemon juice makes it slightly bitter – lemons are funny like that – which is not in the spirit of this cake at all. This is why I recommend that you dissolve the sugar in water and add the juice only once the liquid is cool.

• The pricking of the cake is rather an important aspect of this recipe. A fork is not as good as the skewer, which reaches the bottom of the tin so that the cake is soaked through. Make it 50 pricks rather than 5 . . .

• I have chosen granulated sugar to sprinkle on the top of the cake because I love the crunch, but go ahead with caster if that's what you happen to have.

• I think it's a nice idea to serve in the tin, so perhaps cook this cake in your Sunday Best loaf tin, rather than the one you've been meaning to throw out for twelve years.

BLACKBERRY JAM

BLACKBERRY IS WOOL, walks and stout, stone walls. This jam is the prickly hedgerow world of Wiltshire, where the air smells of mist and damp leaves.

MAKES 1.5 LITRES

900g **blackberries**
900ml water
900g jam sugar (with added pectin; also called preserving sugar)

YOU WILL NEED
four jam jars with lids
a timer

1 Preheat the oven to 100°C/200°F/gas mark ¼.

2 Rinse the blackberries and drain in a colander. Put them in a large saucepan with the water and bring to the boil. Turn down the heat and simmer the fruit with the water gently for 40 minutes uncovered, until quite soft.

3 After 20 minutes of the fruit softening on the hob, sprinkle the sugar over a baking sheet and place it in the oven for 20 minutes.

4 Once the sugar is warmed, remove it from the oven and replace it with the jam jars, with their lids separately. Putting them into the oven sterilizes them and warms them so that the glass doesn't crack under the pressure of the hot jam. Remove the jars from the oven after 20 minutes of warming, ready for the finished jam.

5 Add the warmed sugar (which will make the house smell of candyfloss) to the fruit in the saucepan. Stir until the sugar has dissolved on the low heat that the pan is already sitting over – this takes 5 minutes or so. Once there are no little gritty crystals of sugar under your spoon, bring to the boil. Boil fast for 12 minutes exactly. Spoon off any light-coloured scum that appears on the surface.

6 Spoon the jam carefully into the jars and put their lids on tightly. Leave to cool for an hour before tasting.

PORT MARY SCONES For Betty

THESE SCONES ARE a gang of happy, tired children with wild crimson cheeks and coarse woollen socks and shorts. If they are looking a bit untidy and rugged, it's because they have been rambling and scrambling through the heather with the huge blue sky above them, the whipping wind in their hair and bits of canary gorse clinging to their thick jumpers.

MAKES 8

180g white spelt flour, plus a little extra for rolling and dusting
40g unsalted butter, cold and cubed
¼ tsp salt
2 tsp baking powder
½ tsp bicarbonate of soda
10 scratches of nutmeg or ½ tsp ground nutmeg
200g topped, tailed, peeled and finely grated **courgette**
1 tsp clear honey
40g sultanas
40g glacé cherries, roughly chopped
40g porridge oats (rolled jumbo ones are best)

FOR THE FILLING

1 quantity Sharpie Strawberry Jam (see page 7) or other good-quality shop-bought jam
clotted cream or butter

YOU WILL NEED

a 6cm pastry-cutter
a food processor

1 Preheat the oven to 220°C/425°F/gas mark 7 and line a baking sheet with baking parchment. Lightly brush the parchment with a little vegetable oil.

2 In a food processor, blend the flour with the butter, salt, baking powder, bicarbonate of soda and nutmeg, until fully combined and forming very fine breadcrumbs. Add the grated courgette and honey, and whizz again. This time you will arrive at a stage resembling damp dough. Don't worry that it really is quite damp, as you will be adding flour when you knead in the other dry ingredients.

3 Tip the dough on to a clean, floured surface. Sprinkle the remaining ingredients (sultanas, cherries and oats) over it. Gently knead in these ingredients, as well as enough flour to make a soft and squidgy dough (4–5 tbsp on the work surface should be plenty). The dough shouldn't feel at all wet but should be very flexible to handle.

4 Roll out gently (without pressing too hard) on a floured surface to roughly 5cm thick. Cut out eight circles and place them on the baking sheet. Dust the tops with a little extra flour and cook in the oven for **15 minutes** until risen and golden.

5 Now I don't care what anyone says, there is nothing like a bit of clotted cream and strawberry jam to go with these. If you are feeling virtuous (or strong-willed), a bit of low-fat crème fraîche is not a bad substitute. Like all scones, they are at their tip-top best when eaten warm from the oven, but they will also freeze very well too. Store in an airtight tin.

Port Mary Scones, Sharpie Strawberry Jam

Lemon, Sunflower Seed and Blueberry Muffins

THESE LITTLE LOVES are desperate for the teacher to ask them, so sure are they that they have the right answer. Although a little tiring at times, there is something reassuring about their bright presence in the front row every day.

MAKES 8

2 large unwaxed lemons
3 medium free-range
    eggs
160g caster sugar
250g topped, tailed,
    peeled and finely
    grated **courgette**
180g white rice flour
160g ground almonds
2 tsp baking powder
½ tsp bicarbonate of soda
¼ tsp salt
60g sunflower seeds
150g blueberries

YOU WILL NEED

a 12-hole muffin tray
8 muffin cases (see
    page xxvii for exact
    size)

1 Preheat the oven to 180°C/350°F/gas mark 4 and line the muffin tray with paper cases.

2 Finely grate the lemon zest on to a plate.

3 Beat the eggs and sugar with an electric beater for a full 3 minutes until pale and creamy coloured. Add the grated courgette and lemon zest and beat again. Set the beaters aside. With the help of a spatula, beat in the flour, ground almonds, baking powder, bicarbonate of soda and salt until they are all mixed in. It is important to work as quickly as you can here. Equally fast, add the sunflower seeds and the blueberries. Give it all a good firm stir.

4 Spoon the mixture into the paper cases so that the mixture (which will be quite lumpy and stiff) comes right up to the top of each case. Place in the middle of the oven for **35 minutes**.

5 Take the muffins out of the oven and cool on a wire rack. Don't be afraid of a blueberry-stained and slightly cracked muffin top – this is how I like mine to look.

TRUST ME TIPS

• The key to successful muffins lies in two important aspects. The first is not to overwork or overbeat the mixture. This is why I suggest using a spatula and working really fast once the eggs and sugar have benefited from their 'air and stability workout' with the electric beaters. The second is to have the muffins in a really hot oven in order to encourage them upwards as soon as they enter the heat. So don't leave the oven door open whilst you are fiddling around with the baking tray, or great clouds of heat will spill out. Instead, have everything all nice and ready so that you can pop them in quickly.

CINNAMON BANANA BREAD

THIS CAKE IS so virtuous it's almost geeky. Full of energy, flavour and goodness, it's also a doddle to make.

SERVES 8

140g banana (peeled weight; roughly 1 large one)
2 medium free-range eggs
140g golden caster sugar
150g topped, tailed, peeled and finely grated **courgette**
150g rice flour
2 tsp baking powder
¼ tsp salt
1 tsp vanilla extract
1 tsp cinnamon
½ tsp mixed spice
25g brazil nuts, finely chopped
25g pecans, finely chopped

YOU WILL NEED
a 19cm x 12cm x 8cm (1.7 litre) loaf tin

1 Preheat the oven to 180°C/350°F/gas mark 4. Brush the inside of the loaf tin with a little vegetable oil.

2 Mash the banana thoroughly with a fork.

3 In a large mixing bowl whisk the eggs and sugar for a full 3 minutes until pale and light. Whisk in the mashed-up banana until completely incorporated. Add the grated courgette and beat again. Finally, add the flour, baking powder, salt, vanilla extract, cinnamon and mixed spice, and whisk again until completely blended.

4 Finally, mix in most of the brazil nuts and pecans with a spatula and pour the mixture into the prepared tin. Sprinkle the remaining nuts over the top and bake in the middle of the oven for **45 minutes**.

5 Remove the cake from the oven and leave it to cool in the tin for 10 minutes.

TRUST ME TIPS

• The flavour of the banana will spread out best when it's really well mashed up.

• It is worth chopping the nuts up quite small to make sure that they are evenly spread throughout the cake and that they don't weigh it down too much (this is a particularly light kind of cake).

PISTACHIO CHOCOLATE CAKE

COURGETTE AND CHOCOLATE are an unlikely match, yet they are strangely made for one another, since they combine sensible shoes with dark flashing eyes. As ever, Courgette has pre-booked the taxi at the end of the night to take Chocolate home. And Pistachio stands for Party.

SERVES 12

100g pistachios (shelled)
3 medium free-range
    eggs
180g light Muscovado
    sugar
300g topped, tailed,
    peeled and very
    finely grated
    courgette
120g white rice flour
60g good-quality cocoa
    powder
2 tsp baking powder
¼ tsp salt

FOR THE ICING

1 quantity Naughty
    Chocolate Icing
    (see page 101)
a handful (roughly 25g)
    of pistachios,
    roughly chopped,
    plus another handful
    of whole nuts

YOU WILL NEED

two 18cm-diameter
    x 5cm-deep
    loose-bottomed tins
a food processor

1 Preheat the oven to 180°C/350°F/gas mark 4. Line the tins with baking parchment and brush a little vegetable oil around the base and sides.

2 Blitz the pistachios in the bowl of the food processor until they resemble powder – or as close as you can get to this. If they clog together too much, add a tablespoon of the flour to help them skate around the bowl. Please take all the time required to reach powder, since this will dramatically impact on the texture of the cake.

3 Whisk the eggs and sugar in a large mixing bowl for 2 full minutes until pale and fluffy. Beat in the grated courgette and the pistachio dust, followed by the flour, cocoa powder, baking powder and salt. Beat again to make sure that all the ingredients are mixed together well.

4 Pour evenly into both tins before placing them in the middle of the oven for **30 minutes**.

5 To make the icing, follow the recipe for Naughty Chocolate Icing on page 101. Leave it in the fridge until the cakes are cold.

6 When the cakes are cooked, remove them from the oven and turn them out on to a wire rack. Peel off the baking parchment and leave them to cool for 15 minutes. Refrigerate for another 15 minutes to make quite sure that they are perfectly cold before icing them, otherwise the icing will run off.

7 Lightly ice the underside of both cakes. Sprinkle the bottom one with the whole pistachios before bringing them together and icing the top. Finish off by sprinkling with the chopped pistachios. Store in the fridge and take out 20 minutes before serving.

CONTINUED OVERLEAF

• The pistachios really need to be thoroughly whizzed up in a food processor, since the consistency of the nuts wants to be as similar to dust as possible. Bashing them in a plastic bag till you get powder and chunks is not the same!

• It is crucial to ice the cakes when cold, rather than lukewarm. There is a surprising amount of warmth inside a cool cake, and the icing, which is very light and contains butter, will literally slide off in liquid fashion, which is a disaster.

• The palaver about icing both undersides of the cake separately then adding the whole pistachios is all about the wow factor of finding little nuggets of bright green in the centre of the dark, dark cake. Of course, it's totally up to you if you can't be bothered, but it is rather a breathtaking little dash of colour . . .

NAUGHTY CHOCOLATE ICING

EVERYONE NEEDS A brilliant stand-by chocolate icing for bald cakes or cupcakes . . . Quick and easy, it's also just completely delicious.

MAKES ENOUGH TO ICE 10 CUPCAKES OR 1 WHOLE CAKE

100g unsalted butter, cubed and cold
100g golden icing sugar, sieved
2 tbsp boiling water
50g good-quality cocoa powder

YOU WILL NEED

a hand-held electric whisk

1 In a large mixing bowl, whisk the butter until pale and softened before adding the icing sugar and water. Whisk again until you reach a paste, then beat for a full minute with an electric whisk until doubled in volume.

2 Add the cocoa powder one tablespoon at a time, making sure to stop the beaters whilst you add it or it will simply fly around the room. Once all the cocoa powder is incorporated, beat thoroughly for a final minute until the mixture is full of air and fluff.

3 Before using, make sure that the cake you are going to ice is completely cold. If not using immediately, cover the surface of the icing with cling film and set aside.

TRUST ME TIPS

• If you find it difficult to come by a good chocolate buttercream icing, this one's for you.

• Really beat the butter properly – it will go further and taste lighter and fluffier that way.

• This icing is particularly well suited to a light sponge, since it is rather rich and indulgent. The obvious choices are chocolate sponges but it would also suit a fat-free sponge such as American Vanilla Cupcakes (page 143) very well, or make a nice change in Birthday Cake (page 2) providing you take the lemon zest out of the sponge.

Coconut, Lime and Blueberry Slice, Blueberry Cordial

COCONUT, LIME AND BLUEBERRY SLICE

WITH ITS SUNKEN, drunken blueberries and shot of lime, this cake is loaded with Australian morning light.

SERVES 9

FOR THE BASE

80g caster sugar
20g unsalted butter
pinch of salt
150g desiccated coconut

FOR THE SPONGE

2 medium free-range
    eggs
150g caster sugar
150g topped, tailed,
    peeled and finely
    grated **courgette**
zest and juice of 2
    whole limes
120g white rice flour
2 tsp baking powder
¼ tsp salt
200g blueberries

FOR THE TOP

a little icing sugar

YOU WILL NEED

a 22cm-square x 5cm-
    deep brownie tin

1 Preheat the oven to 180°C/350°F/gas mark 4. Line the base of the tin with baking parchment and brush this and the sides with a little vegetable oil.

2 To make the base, slowly heat the sugar, butter and salt in a saucepan. Within a few minutes the butter will have melted and there will be a sweet paste in the pan. Put the coconut in a large mixing bowl, tip this paste over it and fold together with a palette knife. Treating the mixture like shortcrust pastry, finish combining it with your fingertips. Don't worry that it appears flecked, this will right itself in the oven.

3 Pat the mixture into the tin with a spatula and place it in the oven for **15 minutes**. This should give you just the right amount of time to go ahead with making the sponge, but always keep a keen eye on it, as coconut and sugar love to burn.

4 To make the sponge, beat the eggs and sugar together until light and pale. Add the grated courgette and lime zest, and beat again. Finally, add the flour, baking powder, salt and lime juice, and beat until fully incorporated.

5 Remove the base from the oven and pour the sponge mixture over it, before scattering the blueberries over the top. Cook for a further **30 minutes** in the middle of the oven.

6 Once cooked, cool in its tin for 10 minutes. Sieve icing sugar over the top and cut the cake inside the tin before serving. This cake is gorgeous either on its own or with a scoop of coconut or vanilla ice cream.

BLUEBERRY CORDIAL

THIS CORDIAL IS TWELVE YEARS OLD going on sixty-four. He doesn't care about appearing uncool when he goes fishing with his grandfather. He loves the swishing of the line as it whips through the air, and building smoke boxes to cook the trout that they catch on the river.

MAKES 700ML

600g fresh **blueberries**
freshly squeezed juice
    of 4 lemons
450g caster sugar
400ml water

YOU WILL NEED
one or more glass
    bottle(s) with lid(s)

1 Start by sterilizing the glass bottle in which you plan to keep the cordial. Preheat the oven to 100°C/200°F/gas mark ¼. Place the bottle in the oven, with its lid by its side, when you start making the recipe. Remove from the oven just before using. Don't worry if the cordial sizzles a tiny bit when going in – that's quite normal.

2 Place the blueberries in a large saucepan and strain the lemon juice over them through a sieve. Bring this mixture to the boil and simmer gently for 15 minutes until all the fruit has lost its shape, and all that is left in the saucepan is blue juice and bits of blueberry skin.

3 Pass this through a fine-mesh sieve, one heaped tablespoon at a time. By all means press down hard on it with the back of a spoon. I find that it helps to scoop it up and spread it over the wire a few times. With a clean spoon, scoop up the juice and pulp that has gathered underneath the sieve and let that fall into the blue mixture.

4 When you're quite sure that you've squeezed every ounce of juice from the blueberries, discard the leftover bits of skin in the sieve and repeat the process until you've used up all the mixture. You will obtain somewhere in the region of 300ml of bright purple juice. Set this aside whilst you make the sugar syrup.

5 Start by dissolving the sugar with the water in a saucepan on a low heat until all the sugar crystals have disappeared completely. Bring to the boil and boil hard for 5 minutes (start timing only when you have the mixture boiling hard). The bubbles will creep up the sides of the pan, so don't go anywhere, but rather keep a sharp eye on what's going on inside the pan. It's best not to leave the pan at all during the sugar-syrup stage of this recipe. It's all too easy for the sugar syrup to crystallize – and that's something to avoid at all costs.

6 The clear sugar bubbles will start small, but will grow steadily until they reach the size of transparent walnuts just before the syrup is ready, so watch out for them changing. During the sugar-syrup-making stage, it is important to resist the temptation to stir or fiddle with the pan in any way, as the bubbles will take revenge by crystallizing. Cleaning a pan with crystallized sugar in it is horrid!

7 It is possible, and rather necessary, however, to test the sugar syrup to check what stage it is at. To do this, simply use a metal spoon you have held in your hand for 5 seconds to warm it up, and dip the back of the spoon quickly into the mixture. Bring it out and wait for 5 seconds to see if the liquid runs off. You will have reached the correct sugar-syrup stage when the mixture gently coats the back of the spoon.

8 As soon as you get to this point, remove the pan from the heat and let it stand for 10 minutes. Not only will this prevent the sugar syrup from galloping ahead of itself and going too far, but it will cool and thicken it just enough to syrupify the blueberry juice and bring the cordial together.

9 Once the syrup has cooled for the correct amount of time, add the strained blueberry juice and mix well. Decant into a sterilized bottle and put on the lid. Once opened, store in the fridge. Dilute one part cordial to four parts water.

LAVENDER CUPCAKES

THIS CUPCAKE IS A MOTHER, and a girl. Her hair is as white as a cloud and her eyes are green and twinkling. She loves dressing up in hats, Easter egg hunts, decorating the table with ribbon, and picking wild flowers.

MAKES 12

1 tbsp dried lavender
    flowers
2 medium free-range
    eggs
160g caster sugar
220g topped, tailed,
    peeled and finely
    grated **courgette**
1 tsp vanilla extract
100g white rice flour
120g ground almonds
2 tsp baking powder
¼ tsp salt

FOR THE ICING

140g icing sugar
3 tbsp water
a little purple food
    colouring paste
    (see page 180
    for stockists)

FOR THE TOP

a few extra lavender
    flowers

YOU WILL NEED

a 12-hole muffin tray
12 cupcake cases (see
    page xxvii for
    exact size)

1 Preheat the oven to 180°C/350°F/gas mark 4 and line the muffin tray with the paper cases.

2 Using a pestle and mortar, bash up the lavender flowers and tip them on to a plate.

3 Whisk the eggs and sugar in a large mixing bowl for 5 minutes, until pale and quadrupled in volume. Add the grated courgette and vanilla extract, and whisk again. Mix in the crushed flowers, flour, ground almonds, baking powder and salt. Whisk to combine.

4 Spoon the mixture into the paper cases, aiming for it to come four fifths of the way up each case. Place in the oven for **20 minutes** until risen and cooked. Don't be alarmed that they are flat on the top rather than dome shaped.

5 Whilst the cupcakes are cooking, make the icing. Sieve the icing sugar into a small mixing bowl. Add the water and colouring, a tiny bit at a time with the tip of a toothpick in order to control the colour. Stir with a fork till you are looking at a lavender-coloured paste. Beware of spots of colouring that are lurking and will suddenly turn the colour a lot darker. If not using straight away, place a sheet of cling film directly over the surface of the icing, and keep until needed.

6 Once cooked, remove the cakes from the oven and cool them in the tin for 15 minutes. Once cold, ice each cupcake and decorate with a few scattered lavender flowers.

Cake Diaries

LEMON AND LAVENDER DRIZZLE CAKE

Testing Number 3: 29 September
I was a clot and didn't write up my recipe properly last time, which is why I tested it again and added the final touches . . . Perfect this time. Just like Mary Poppins.

PORT MARY SCONES

Testing Number 2: 5 November
This recipe is an old friend (at least five months old, I'm guessing). I've tried it with turnip and the mechanics were perfect (which is what I was road testing above all) but the flavour was horrid. Number two is now in the oven with darling courgette and I can't see what on earth could prevent the scones from tasting like little Scottish clouds . . . Done. They're all ready to go out and play.

LEMON, SUNFLOWER SEED AND BLUEBERRY MUFFINS

Testing Number 5: 25 November
Gosh, only a month till Christmas Day . . . I'm really quite cross with parsnip today. It may be pale but it's certainly not innocent. I switched the courgette for parsnip because the first batch came out flat, dense, disgruntled and like dumpy little muffins. I'm all rattled now and won't stop until I beat this one into shape. The re-test will have to wait as I'm out of blueberries, sunflower seeds and patience.

Testing Number 6: 26 November
Well, there's a serious improvement. We have arrived – mmmm . . .

CINNAMON BANANA BREAD

Testing Number 1: 12 April
So nearly a hole in one! This is such a good cake. She's full of helpful and healthy ingredients. Bound to become such a good friend. She's a little on the tight side at the moment. Up with the flour a notch, and more spice.

Testing Number 2: 12 April
This is such a hit with Polly and Tom! We've arrived.

COCONUT CAKE WITH COCONUT ICING

Testing Number 1: 25 November
This is a cake with a big bottom. I doubt very much if she has a spiteful side, but I will find out . . . No spite, I'm pleased to report.

Testing Number 2: 25 November
She is so happy, with a lovely damp texture and a beautiful, generous outlook on life. All she wants now is a hammock and a cold, peach drink.

ROSEWATER FAIRY
CAKES

ROSEWATER FAIRY CAKES

THESE LITTLE GIRLS are completely over the top: the lip-gloss version of the Bennet sisters, they giggle all the time.

MAKES 12

2 medium free-range eggs
160g caster sugar
250g topped, tailed,
    peeled and finely
    grated **courgette**
finely grated zest of
    1 lemon
1 tbsp rose water
100g white rice flour
100g ground almonds
2 tsp baking powder
¼ tsp salt

FOR THE ICING
1 quantity of Snow
    Meringue Icing
    (see page 85),
    replacing 1 tbsp
    water with 1 tbsp
    rose water
pink or red food
    colouring paste
    (see page 180 for
    stockists)

FOR THE TOP
pink roses, red
    geraniums, sugared
    rose petals, fresh
    flower petals, pink
    sprinkles . . .

YOU WILL NEED
a 12-hole muffin tray
12 cupcake cases (see
    page xxvii for exact
    size)

1 Preheat the oven to 180°C/350°F/gas mark 4 and line the muffin tray with the paper cases.

2 Whisk the eggs and the sugar for 5 minutes until pale and precocious, and full of air and graces. Whisk in the grated courgette, lemon zest and rose water. Next add the flour, ground almonds, baking powder and salt, and beat to combine.

3 Ladle the mixture evenly between the paper cases, so that it comes four fifths of the way up the sides. Bake for **30 minutes**.

4 Remove the cakes from the oven and cool on a wire rack whilst you make the icing.

5 To make the icing, follow the recipe for Snow Meringue Icing (see page 85). It's entirely up to you how much or how little rose water you want to put in. Just remember that the total amount of liquid should not exceed 2 tablespoons.

6 Run a tiny amount of food colouring on the end of a toothpick through the mixture until you get to the shade that you want. And I really mean a tiny bit!

7 Ice the cupcakes straight away with a palette knife or spatula. They should end up looking like the pink version of a '99 flake ice cream . . .

TRUST ME TIPS

• Be careful to use rose water and not rose essence, which is much stronger. Most people (including me) can't handle too much rose water because it's a bit like eating soap. I love it once in a while, but feel that a little goes a long way . . . let's say, all the way to the sandy deserts of the Arabian Nights . . .

• Red food colouring works well too, as long as you remember that you only need an ant's amount for a bowl of icing – especially if you dream of candyfloss pink cupcakes (as I do).

LIME AND GINGER BARLEY WATER

THIS YOUNG MAN came back from six months' travelling, totally changed. He used to be tidy, but he now has long hair and a couple of tattoos, and he's changed his name to something cool. Lime and Ginger is so striking that his mother didn't recognize him when she came to pick him up from the airport.

MAKES 1.4 LITRES

100g pearl barley, rinsed
under the tap
80g raw ginger, peeled
and finely sliced
2.4 litres water
120g palm sugar
freshly squeezed juice of
12 limes (roughly
400ml)

YOU WILL NEED

one or more glass
bottle(s) with lid(s)

1 Preheat the oven to 100°C/200°F/gas mark ¼. Place the bottle, with its lid separately, in the oven to sterilize. Remove just before using.

2 Put the rinsed barley and ginger into a large saucepan. Add the water and bring to the boil. Simmer the mixture on a very low heat for 1 hour. The water should be shimmering (as if excited at what is going on), but by no means boiling. If you look into the pan, the ginger should be hovering mysteriously in the water and the odd pearl of barley leaping up from the deep. Anything more energetic than this means the heat is too high.

3 Strain the mixture through a sieve, discarding the ginger and barley. Add the sugar and stir to dissolve for a minute or so until no sugar crystals are left. Because palm sugar is so coarse and has such big crystals (unless you are using it in paste form, in which case the following doesn't apply), you will probably need to heat it up gently for a couple of minutes to dissolve it completely.

4 Add the lime juice through a sieve to the sweet ginger barley water.

5 Pour into the bottle with a few shreds of ginger before sealing the top. Store in the fridge until needed. It will keep for up to a month. Dilute one part barley water to one part water.

TRUST ME TIPS

• I have used palm sugar because it gives a lovely, rich flavour and is in tune with the other ingredients. Feel free to replace with Demerara or golden caster sugar if you have trouble finding palm sugar.

• This is really refreshing with vodka and vermouth if you want a martini mixer.

• Don't be alarmed that the barley water is a scruffy, cloudy colour – that's why his mother got such a shock!

ST CLEMENT'S CUPCAKES

THESE CUPCAKES ARE Tudor schoolgirls, skipping through the City of London singing 'Oranges and lemons say the bells of St Clement's'. They are light and carefree (considering the solemn times), with cheeky citrus personalities and a good dose of defiance.

MAKES 12

3 medium free-range
    eggs
160g caster sugar
200g peeled and finely
    grated **pumpkin** or
    butternut squash
finely grated zest of 2
    oranges (juicing
    varieties, such as
    Seville, are best)
finely grated zest of
    2 unwaxed lemons
150g white rice flour
50g ground almonds
2 tsp baking powder
¼ tsp salt

FOR THE ICING

200 icing sugar
1 tbsp freshly squeezed
    lemon juice
2 tbsp freshly squeezed
    orange juice

FOR THE TOP

orange and yellow
    flowers

YOU WILL NEED

a 12-hole muffin tray
12 cupcake cases (see
    page xxvii for exact
    size)

1 Preheat the oven to 180°C/350°F/gas mark 4. Line the muffin tray with the paper cases.

2 In a largish mixing bowl, beat the eggs and sugar for 5 minutes until pale and fluffy. Whisk in the grated pumpkin and the orange and lemon zests, followed by the flour, ground almonds, baking powder and salt, and beat for another minute.

3 Ladle the mixture into the cases so that it comes four fifths of the way up the sides. Place in the middle of the oven for **30 minutes**.

4 Remove the cakes from the oven and cool on a wire rack for 15 minutes whilst you make the icing.

5 To make the icing, sieve the icing sugar into a large bowl. Put the lemon and orange juice into another bowl. Using a measuring spoon, measure out 2 tbsp juice into the sieved sugar and mix together with a fork. If not using the icing immediately, place a sheet of cling film directly over the surface to prevent it drying out.

6 Spoon the thick icing on to the cupcakes. Finally, decorate with orange and yellow flowers.

TRUST ME TIPS

• Please choose imperfect, large and knobbly looking lemons over those mean, tight, waxed ones.

• I know it's a faffy way of making the icing (and you are left with some spare juice), but it's important to get a good orange and lemon balance, as well as consistency.

SYRUP SCONES

THESE SCONES ARE good for the soul, and belong with squidgy sofas, the smell of pipe tobacco, the creaking of the stairs, and battered paperback books.

MAKES 7 PERFECT SCONES AND 2 UGLY MUGLIES

250g white spelt flour, plus a little extra for rolling and dusting
1 tsp baking powder
1 tsp bicarbonate of soda
¼ tsp salt
40g unsalted butter, cold and cubed
3 tbsp golden syrup
200g peeled and finely grated **sweet potato**
grated zest of ½ unwaxed lemon

YOU WILL NEED

a 6cm pastry-cutter
a food processor

1 Preheat the oven to 200°C/400°F/gas mark 6 and line a baking sheet with baking parchment. Lightly brush the parchment with a little vegetable oil.

2 Put the flour, baking powder, bicarbonate of soda and salt into the bowl of the food processor, along with the butter. Whizz it until you reach butter-coloured breadcrumbs (they will be very fine).

3 Dip a tablespoon into boiling water for a second and then use it to scoop the golden syrup out of its tin. Pour these spoonfuls into the breadcrumb mixture. Add the grated sweet potato and lemon zest. Pulse until the mixture comes together to form a damp dough.

4 Tip the dough out on to a lightly floured surface, and knead it lightly until it has absorbed enough flour to make it easy to handle. Roll out the dough (aim for about 4cm thickness), taking care not to apply too much pressure.

5 Cut out nine scones with your pastry-cutter and place them on the baking sheet. Dust a little flour over the tops and put into the middle of the oven for **12–15 minutes**, until risen and golden.

6 Serve with clotted cream and warmed golden syrup or Sharpie Strawberry Jam (see page 7).

TRUST ME TIPS

• Please don't be alarmed that the raw dough is a little flexible. Just give it a good roll around and a light knead in the flour before you roll it out. I even prefer patting it flat with my hands rather than using a rolling pin, which I find too heavy and brutal.

• There is a rule with scones: you absolutely must be decisive when you slice them into their shapes. I have tried cutting them with a glass and then wondered why they didn't hurtle upwards in the oven. This is because they only respond to a clean and salient break (like a guillotine), not a push downwards and a wiggle of the glass.

CHERRY AND ALMOND CAKE

THIS CAKE IS EXTREMELY HEADSTRONG. She is the rose belonging to the Little Prince, with a suspicious attitude and four thorns to protect her against the world . . .

SERVES 12

250g glacé cherries
3 medium free-range
    eggs
180g caster sugar
200g finely grated
    potato (such as
    Maris Piper)
100g rice flour, plus
    2 tbsp extra on
    a plate
100g ground almonds
1 tsp almond extract
2 tsp baking powder
¼ tsp salt
very finely grated zest of
    ½ unwaxed lemon
    (finest possible shred)

FOR THE MIDDLE
250g Sour Cherry Jam
    (see page 123) or
    good-quality shop-
    bought cherry jam
    (red cherries rather
    than black as they
    are sharper)

FOR THE TOP
20g almond flakes
1 tbsp icing sugar
¼ tsp cinnamon

YOU WILL NEED
two 18cm-diameter x
    5cm-deep loose-
    bottomed tins

1 Preheat the oven to 180°C/350°F/gas mark 4. Lightly brush the two sandwich tins with a little vegetable oil, then line the bottoms and sides with baking parchment and brush with oil again.

2 Cut all the cherries in half and toss them in the extra 2 tbsp flour until they are lightly coated all over.

3 In a large mixing bowl, whisk together the eggs and sugar for 5 minutes until pale and light.

4 Next, beat in the grated potato until well combined. Finally, add the flour, ground almonds, almond extract, baking powder, salt and lemon zest until well incorporated.

5 Divide the mixture between the two sandwich tins and gently place the cherries on the top of each cake so that they are slightly sunken into the mixture. Place them in the middle of the oven for **30 minutes**.

6 Whilst the cake is cooking, toast the almond flakes in a dry frying pan. Don't even think of leaving them and going to put a stamp on an envelope for a couple of minutes because they will take this opportunity to burn. The only thing to do is patiently wait for the 5 minutes that it takes to turn them from white to tanned. Once toasted, remove them from the pan immediately and put them on a plate.

7 Once cooked, remove the cakes from the oven and unmould them on to a wire rack to cool for 10 minutes. Gently peel off the baking parchment.

8 To assemble the cake, sandwich the cooled cake layers with the cherry jam and sprinkle the top with the toasted almonds. Finally, mix together the icing sugar and cinnamon and sieve liberally over the top.

CONTINUED OVERLEAF

TRUST ME TIPS

- It may well feel like a pain in the neck to line the sides of the tin with baking parchment, but this cake mixture is really quite determined to cling to the edges, which is why I consider it important here.

- Coating the cherries in flour means that they don't sink straight to the bottom of the cake . . .

Raspberry and Elderflower Cupcakes

THESE TWO HAVE BEEN FRIENDS since they were five years old. They embody Englishness in all its polite reticence. When asked a question, they defer to the other: 'No, you go first.' 'No, no, you go.' In the end, you never get a straight answer from either of them!

MAKES 12

2 medium free-range
    eggs
140g caster sugar
200g topped, tailed,
    peeled and finely
    grated **courgette**
3 tbsp elderflower
    cordial
80g white rice flour
120g ground almonds
2 tsp baking powder
¼ tsp salt
120g fresh raspberries,
    plus 12 extra ones
    for the tops

FOR THE ICING

140g icing sugar
3 tbsp elderflower
    cordial
a little pink food
    colouring paste
    (optional) (see page
    180 for stockists)

YOU WILL NEED

a 12-hole muffin tray
12 cupcake cases (see
    page xxvii for exact
    size)

1 Preheat the oven to 180°C/350°F/gas mark 4 and line the muffin tray with the paper cases.

2 Whisk the eggs and sugar in a large mixing bowl for 5 minutes, until pale and quadrupled in volume.

3 Add the grated courgette and the elderflower cordial, and whisk again. Mix in the flour, ground almonds, baking powder and salt until they are well introduced. Gently fold in the raspberries, taking care not to crush them up too much.

4 Spoon the mixture into the cupcake cases, aiming for it to come four fifths of the way up each case. Place in the oven for **25 minutes** until risen and cooked. Don't be alarmed that they are flat on the top rather than dome shaped – this is perfectly normal.

5 Whilst the cupcakes are cooking, make the icing. Sieve the icing sugar into a small mixing bowl. Add the elderflower cordial and mix it in with a fork until it forms a loose white icing. Add the colouring (if using), a tiny bit at a time with the tip of a toothpick in order to control the colour. If not using straight away, place a sheet of cling film directly over the surface of the icing to prevent it drying out and keep until needed.

6 Once the cakes are cooked, remove them from the oven and cool in the tin for 15 minutes. Ice each cupcake individually and decorate with a raspberry.

Vanilla Cream and Raspberry Swiss Roll

This Swiss roll has rosy cheeks and loves food. She starts thinking of Easter as soon as Christmas is over . . .

SERVES 8

a little icing sugar
100g caster sugar
¼ tsp salt
4 medium free-range
  eggs, yolks and
  whites separated
1 vanilla pod, split
  lengthways and
  seeds scraped out
100g peeled and finely
  grated **sweet
  potato**
70g white rice flour
1 tsp baking powder
caster sugar for dusting
  over the top

FOR THE FILLING

2 tbsp icing sugar, sieved
1 tsp vanilla extract
140ml double cream
200g Seedless Raspberry
  Jam (see page 126)
  or good-quality shop-
  bought jam
100g fresh raspberries

YOU WILL NEED

a 33cm x 24cm x 2cm
  Swiss roll tin
a rubber spatula
a clean tea towel

1 Preheat the oven to 180°C/350°F/gas mark 4. Line the base of the Swiss roll tin with baking parchment, cutting into the corners to get a neat fit. Using a sieve, sprinkle this with icing sugar so that there is a fine layer more or less all over the base. This is important in helping prevent the sponge from sticking to the bottom.

2 Measure the caster sugar into a small mixing bowl with the salt. Now remove 2 tbsp of the sugar and put them into a large mixing bowl with the egg whites. Whisk until the egg whites are stiff. Set the large mixing bowl aside.

3 Add the vanilla seeds and egg yolks to the remaining sugar in the smaller mixing bowl and whisk for a full 4 minutes until they are pale, fluffy and hold a ribbon trail when you lift the beaters. Add the sweet potato to the egg-yolk mixture and whisk to incorporate.

4 With the help of a rubber spatula, beat one third of the egg whites into the egg-yolk mixture. Don't be shy, you needn't be afraid of hurting the sponge at this stage.

5 Taking care to work delicately so as not to knock out too much of the air, cautiously fold in the next third of egg whites. To do this, spoon the egg white into the middle of the bowl, so that it is sitting on the bubbly mixture, then go under the contents of the bowl with your spatula as if you were cleaning the sides, and dump the liquid from the bottom on to the floating egg-white island in the middle of the bowl. Then, decisively cut through the middle of the floating egg white with the side of your spatula and repeat the process until it has broken up and blended in an airy pillow with the heavier liquid part.

6 Repeat the process with the final third of egg white and, at the same time, sieve the flour and baking powder into the mixture. Fold as before until all elements are incorporated.

7 Pour the mixture carefully into the prepared Swiss roll tin, aiming to drag the lazy mixture from the bowl into the centre of the tin. This makes it easier to tilt the tin this way and that to coax the

CONTINUED OVERLEAF

mixture into the corners of the tin, so that it doesn't just lie in the centre. Don't pat it down with the spatula as this will knock out the air completely. It is important for the mixture to reach all corners of the tin because the mixture will set and start to cook very soon after it has gone into the oven because it is so flat and exposed. How it goes into the tin is how it will end up looking once cooked.

8 Cook in the middle of the oven for **15 minutes**. Once cooked, it is important to act quickly. Lay a clean tea towel flat on an empty kitchen surface and cover it with a slightly smaller rectangle of baking parchment of the same shape.

9 Take the tray out of the oven and carefully lift the sponge out of its tin, holding it with the edges of the baking parchment. Don't be frightened by the sponge that is clinging to the paper; it is quite safe and much more robust than you think.

10 Place the sponge, exposed side down, on the baking parchment in the middle of the tea towel (lay it out lengthways so that it looks like two rectangles that fit into each other) and carefully peel off the paper from the back of the cooked sponge; it will come off easily in your hands.

11 The next stage is the most important of all. Start from one end of the cloth and roll a cigar shape with the tea towel and parchment paper. When you come to the sponge, continue to roll it snugly, so that the sponge and the towel are meshed together in a roly-poly shape. Continue until all the sponge is cosily tucked up inside the tea towel. Let it stand for 10 minutes to cool and semi-set in a snail shape whilst you make the vanilla cream filling.

12 Beat the icing sugar, vanilla extract and cream for 1 minute on full blast until stiff. As always, don't over-whip the cream or it will go grainy and split and splutter. Put it away in the fridge until needed.

13 Once the sponge has had 10 minutes to cool off and slightly set, unroll it from its paper and tea towel, and spread a generous layer of Seedless Raspberry Jam or jam all over the inside. Remove the cream from the fridge and spread it over the top of the raspberry layer. Sprinkle over the fresh raspberries.

14 Roll the bulging sponge up again and don't worry about the mess. It's bound to crack a little here and overspill a little there. Scatter the caster sugar all over the top and refrigerate until needed. Take the Swiss roll out 10 minutes before serving for a lighter result.

Sour Cherry Jam

ALTHOUGH SOUR IN TASTE, this old bird is far too wise and crinkled about the eyes to be sour in life. A glossy dollop of Sour Cherry Jam is wonderful with any hard sheep's or goat's cheese to ease you into autumn in the Pays Basque.

MAKES 1.3 LITRES

1.6kg pitted **cherries** (roughly 1.9kg fresh cherries)

400ml freshly squeezed lemon juice (roughly 7 medium lemons)

400ml water

500g jam sugar (with added pectin; also called preserving sugar)

YOU WILL NEED

four or five jam jars with lids

a cherry-pitter (or a small knife and a lot of patience)

a timer

1 Preheat the oven to 100°C/200°F/gas mark ¼.

2 When you have pitted the cherries, place them in a very large saucepan. Strain the lemon juice through a sieve into the saucepan with the cherries and the water. Bring to the boil and simmer very slowly for **1 hour**, uncovered. Remember to scrape off gently, with a metal spoon, any pale-coloured scum that forms on the surface.

3 Whilst the cherries are gently bubbling away, place the jam jars, with their lids separately, in the oven for 20 minutes to sterilize them and warm them so that the glass doesn't crack under the pressure of the hot jam. Take them out 10 minutes before the jam is finished.

4 Whilst sterilizing the jars, warm the sugar on a baking tray in the low heat of the oven for the last 20 minutes of the cherries' bubbling time.

5 Add the warmed sugar to the pan and stir the mixture (still on the lowest possible heat) for 3–4 minutes, or until you are sure that no gritty bits of sugar crystals are lying at the bottom of the pan.

6 Once all the sugar has dissolved, bring the mixture to the boil. As it reaches full boil, set your timer for 12 minutes exactly. Remember to stir the mixture (going right into the corners of the pan) every couple of minutes to prevent the jam from sticking to the bottom and burning.

7 Once the 12 minutes are up, carefully pour the hot jam into the prepared jars and put the lids on so that they are sealed tightly shut. Leave to cool and set for an hour before tasting.

Coconut Cake with Coconut icing

THIS JOLLY CAKE has never been on a diet in her life, and her infectious laugh gurgles up from deep inside her bosom. Sometimes life is just too short to count calories . . .

SERVES 10

200g desiccated coconut
3 medium free-range
    eggs
180g caster sugar
250g topped, tailed,
    peeled and very
    finely grated
    courgette
1 tbsp vanilla extract
120g white rice flour
2 tsp baking powder
½ tsp bicarbonate of soda
¼ tsp salt

FOR THE FILLING
½ jar of sharp red jam,
    such as Seedless
    Raspberry Jam
    (see page 126) or
    Sharpie Strawberry
    Jam (see page 7).

FOR THE ICING
2 tbsp coconut milk
100g icing sugar, sieved

FOR THE TOP
small handful of toasted
    coconut shavings

YOU WILL NEED
two 18cm-diameter
    x 5cm-deep loose-
    bottomed tins
a food processor

1 Preheat the oven to 160°C/325°F/gas mark 3. Lightly brush the tins with a little vegetable oil. Line the base and sides with baking parchment, then grease them again all over.

2 Blitz the desiccated coconut in the food processor for 2 minutes. This will shred it slightly finer than it already is, which in turn will help lift the texture of the cake. Set it aside on a plate.

3 Whisk the eggs and sugar till pale and fluffy (4 minutes full blast with a hand-held whisk will give you a good result). Beat in the grated courgette and the vanilla extract.

4 Finally, add the coconut, flour, baking powder, bicarbonate of soda and salt, and beat to combine. Pour the mixture evenly into the two tins and place them in the middle of the oven for **45 minutes**.

5 Remove the cakes from the oven and unmould them. Cool them on a wire rack for 15 minutes whilst you make the icing.

6 To make the icing, pour the coconut milk into the icing sugar and combine them into a loose paste with the help of a spoon. Crush out any lumps with the back of your spoon. Place a little sheet of cling film directly on to the icing to avoid it forming a skin whilst the cakes are cooling.

7 When cool enough to handle (15 minutes out of the oven should be fine), spread the jam or jelly over one cake and sandwich the two together. Pour the icing over so that it covers the top and drips lazily down the sides. Sprinkle the coconut shavings over the top before serving.

• A thin strip of baking parchment the length of the circumference of the tin will work beautifully for lining the sides of the tin. This is to protect the cake from the heat and prevent it from toasting too much (coconut catches very easily).

• The stage involving the blitzing of the coconut flakes is really rather important in helping the cake to be fluffy and light, so please don't skip it unless you just don't have a food processor.

• Coconut shavings aren't always easy to find. If you can't get hold of any but still want some for the top, take the flesh from a whole coconut and shave it with a potato-peeler into long, paper-thin strips.

SEEDLESS RASPBERRY JAM

SEEDLESS RASPBERRY JAM is more set in her ways than she first appears (the bright-red nail polish is deceiving). The turban pinned with a brooch is a wink to her days as an actress, when she lived off oranges and Edam cheese.

MAKES 1 LITRE

1.2kg **raspberries**
1 litre water
1.2kg jam sugar (with added pectin; also called preserving sugar)

YOU WILL NEED

three or four jam jars with lids
a really big saucepan or stock pot
a timer

1 Preheat the oven to 100°C/200°F/gas mark ¼. Place the clean jars, with their lids beside them, into the oven. This will sterilize them and will also warm them so that the glass doesn't crack under pressure from the hot jam. They need only around 20 minutes in the oven, but it won't hurt to put them in now, and this will mean that there is one thing less to forget later on.

2 Rinse the raspberries in a colander under the tap. Bring the fruit and water to the boil in a large saucepan, then turn down the heat and simmer gently for 30 minutes uncovered, stirring every so often to ensure that none of the fruit is burning at the bottom.

3 Meanwhile, spread the sugar on a baking tray and warm it in the oven for 20 minutes alongside the jars.

4 Once the simmering time is up, add the warmed sugar to the pan and stir to dissolve for 5 minutes. Bring to the boil and boil hard for 14 minutes exactly, stirring all the time to make sure that none of the mixture sticks to the bottom of the pan. With the help of a large spoon, remove any pale-coloured scum that appears on the surface of the jam.

5 When the fruit and sugar have had their time, spoon the jam carefully into a sieve over a large, clean mixing bowl. (It is a good idea to pour a little boiling water into the bottom of this bowl in order to sterilize it too.) You may have to do this in batches as it is important not to overfill the sieve.

6 Patiently stir the jam through the sieve, letting the juice fall below while the sieve retains all the pips. Scrape the sieve with a spoon to encourage as much as possible of the raspberry juice through. It will be helpful to empty the sieve of pips before adding the next batch.

7 Once all the raspberries have been passed through the sieve, decant the jam carefully into the sterilized jars and put the lids on. Leave to chill and set in the fridge for at least 2 hours.

Cake Diaries

ST CLEMENT'S CUPCAKES

Testing Number 1: 3 April

It feels good to be handling such vibrant and fresh colours – the pumpkin orange is a positive tonic after all that chocolate and coffee. I'm hoping for a kind recipe that doesn't torture me into a million testings. I've just come out of a chocolate headache and would rather not fly straight into a lemon migraine next . . . Not a bad first attempt at all. The balance of sweet/sharp is good. The texture is a bit too tight so I'm thinking up with the pumpkin. Thank you to the sharp St Clement's girls for a dose of encouragement. I needed this.

Testing Number 3: 3 April

The mixture is much more together, I'm glad to say. Wow, I've hit a wall with the icing though. It wants to be sharp for goodness' sake.

Testing Number 5: 3 April

At last. With the right icing, these cupcakes really are skipping down the alleyways around Threadneedle Street.

CHERRY AND ALMOND CAKE

Testing Number 1: 22 April

Ugh, this girl's got attitude . . . I'm sensing a struggle ahead.

Testing Number 2: 22 April

Very unsubstantial mixture – no weight at all. I'm looking for a more mature crumb.

Testing Number 3: 22 April

This is a new experience . . . I'm confused. This cake wants to be someone completely different! She is telling me she does *not* want to be iced.

Testing Number 4: 26 April

I guess I had better listen and give into her this time – things are not going my way at all! What a *female* I have come across! And the potato is really great and very stable. I reckon these potatoes are men – even these Maris Pipers. Too well behaved to be girls.

Testing Number 5: 27 April

Very interesting indeed. I love the Bakewell vibe here. The fluff is good but we may need more structure . . . After a night's sleep, I think that a handful of rose thorns (cinnamon and icing sugar) is the right topping. Also, a little lemon zest through the cake and a layer of Sour Cherry Jam is the answer.

Testing Number 6: 27 April

She has ended up not at all as I had envisaged her at first: I had seen her as giggly and girly; she is sophisticated and handsome. I imagined her sweet and light; she is complex and sensitive. She so reminds me of the stubborn, vulnerable rose in *The Little Prince* . . . We're here now, and she's just right.

RASPBERRY AND ELDERFLOWER CUPCAKES

Testing Number 1: 20 December

Number eighty! I can't believe I'm here. There were so many times when I wondered what this would feel like (or if I'd ever get here at all!). I'm thrilled with the fluff in this one. It's featherweight stuff. So unexpected and gently with pink cushions and elderflower underwear.

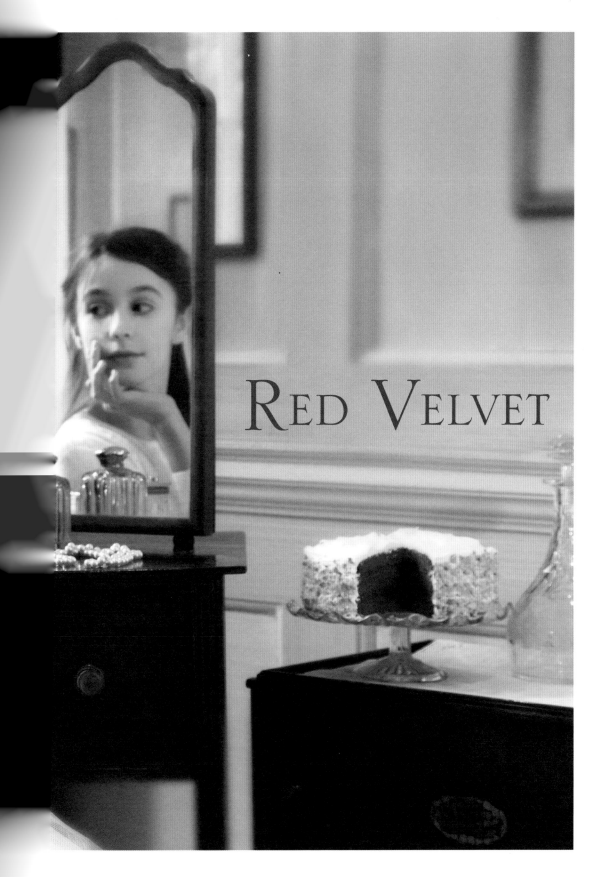

RED VELVET

RED VELVET CAKE

Do you remember gazing in mystified admiration whilst your mother got ready to go out? This cake is the food equivalent of watching her put on her lipstick.

SERVES 12

3 medium free-range eggs
180g caster sugar
200g topped, tailed, peeled and finely grated **beetroot**
1 vanilla pod, split lengthways and seeds scraped out
180g white rice flour
180g ground almonds
2 tsp baking powder
1 tbsp good-quality cocoa powder
¼ tsp salt
284ml buttermilk
1 tsp red food colouring paste (I use Christmas Red; see page 180 for stockists)

FOR THE FILLING
6 tbsp Nutella or other scrumptious chocolate spread

FOR THE ICING
1 quantity Snow Meringue Icing (see page 85)
2 tsp vanilla extract

FOR THE SIDES
120g hazelnuts

YOU WILL NEED
three 18cm-diameter x 5cm-deep loose-bottomed tins

1 Preheat the oven to 160°C/325°F/gas mark 3 and lightly brush the base and sides of the tins with vegetable oil. Line the bases with baking parchment and lightly grease again.

2 Toast the hazelnuts for the sides for 10 minutes on a baking sheet. Please set a timer, or I promise that you'll forget that they're in there! Once toasted, chop them up finely and set them aside for later.

3 In a large mixing bowl, whisk up the eggs and sugar for 4 minutes until they are light and fluffy. Next beat in the grated beetroot, as well as the vanilla seeds from the scraped-out pod. Add the flour, ground almonds, baking powder, cocoa powder and salt, and whisk until well combined.

4 Finally, add the buttermilk and red food colouring. Whisk well to make sure that the elements in the bowl are well introduced and the mixture looks like a prude who's just been told a rude joke.

5 Divide the mixture evenly between the three tins and place them in the middle of the oven for **30 minutes**.

6 When the cakes are cooked, remove them from the oven, unmould and place them on a wire rack for 10 minutes. Peel off the paper and sit them underside up to cool quicker.

7 Use this time to make the Snow Meringue Icing (see page 85), making sure to add the vanilla extract.

8 When the cakes are cold, spread 3 tbsp of the Nutella or other chocolate spread between the first and second tiers of the cake, then another 3 tbsp between the second and third tiers.

9 Cover the whole cake with Snow Meringue Icing, and pat on the toasted, chopped-up hazelnuts. Serve on a cake stand if you have one. This cake keeps for 2 days in a tin or other airtight container.

CONTINUED OVERLEAF

TRUST ME TIPS

• The flamboyance of this cake is at the very heart of its story, which is why I implore you to use paste colouring rather than those dinky little bottles of red liquid. I tried the liquid dye and not only does an unpleasant smell of ammonia come from the warm cake, but the red is pathetic. I'm afraid that if you're going to go for it, you just have to give it the full head of red hair or not bother at all. The colouring is crucial, therefore I recommend Sugarflair Colours, and the hue I prefer is Christmas Red. Poppy Red, Red Extra and Ruby work well too, but stay away from Claret or other darker reds.

CHOCOLATE AND CHERRY BRANDY CUPCAKES

THIS LADY CAN HANDLE HERSELF anywhere. She has a sharp witty tongue and speaks at the speed of the trains that pulse through the East End. She never sleeps alone, and always keeps a bottle of sherry in the flat should anyone come to call.

MAKES 12

2 medium free-range eggs
180g Demerara sugar
200g peeled and grated
  butternut squash
100ml cherry brandy
50g white rice flour
100g ground almonds
50g good-quality cocoa
  powder
2 tsp baking powder
¼ tsp salt
12 tsp cherry jam (such
  as Sour Cherry Jam
  (see page 123) or
  good-quality shop-
  bought jam)

FOR THE ICING

150g icing sugar, sieved
2 tbsp cherry brandy
1 tbsp boiling water
30g good-quality cocoa
  powder
small pinch of salt

FOR THE TOP

12 whole cherries, with
  stems

YOU WILL NEED

a 12-hole muffin tray
12 cupcake cases (see
  page xxvii for exact
  size)

1 Preheat the oven to 180°C/350°F/gas mark 4 and line the muffin tray with the paper cases.

2 Whisk the eggs and sugar in a large mixing bowl for 5 minutes, until pale and quadrupled in volume. Add the grated butternut squash and cherry brandy, then whisk again. Mix in the flour, ground almonds, cocoa powder, baking powder and salt until well combined.

3 Spoon 1 heaped tbsp of the mixture into the bottom of each paper case, followed by 1 tsp of the jam. Fill the rest of the case up with the mixture so that it comes nearly to the top of each case.

4 Place in the middle of the oven for **30 minutes** until the cakes are risen and cooked.

5 Whilst the cupcakes are cooking, make the icing. Combine the icing sugar with the cherry brandy, boiling water and cocoa powder until you have a smooth paste. The back of a spoon works wonders for flattening out lumps. Depending on how absorbent your cocoa powder is, you may need a dash more brandy to loosen the paste enough for spreading evenly. If you are not going to use it immediately, place a sheet of cling film directly on the surface of the icing to prevent it drying out.

6 Remove the cupcakes from the oven and cool them in the tin for 10 minutes, so that they are cold enough to ice. Spread a spoonful of icing evenly over the top of each one and place a whole cherry (with its stem still on) on top of each cupcake before serving.

PARMESAN AND PAPRIKA SCONES

ALWAYS A FAVOURITE with your mum, this scone writes beautiful and amusing thank-you letters. People twitter about a girlfriend somewhere, but no one has ever met her, and it always seems to be a different girl . . .

MAKES 8–10

60g Parmesan, finely grated, plus a little extra for the top
200g peeled and finely grated **butternut squash**
1 heaped tsp clear honey
250g white spelt flour, plus a little extra for rolling
1 tbsp smoked paprika, plus a little extra for the top
2 tsp baking powder
½ tsp bicarbonate of soda
¼ tsp salt
a generous grind of black pepper
3 tbsp water

YOU WILL NEED
a 6cm pastry-cutter
a food processor

1 Preheat the oven to 200°C/400°F/gas mark 6. Line a baking sheet with foil and baking parchment. Lightly dust the parchment with a little flour.

2 Put the Parmesan, grated butternut squash and honey into the bowl of the food processor. Whizz briefly to combine.

3 Next add the flour, paprika, baking powder, bicarbonate of soda, salt and black pepper to the food processor. Pulse until combined. You will go through the following stages: dust and rubble, breadcrumbs (at which point add the water), wet sand, damp dough. Run your knife around the edges, then pulse again until a crumbly dough is formed. It doesn't have to be in one piece – just as long as the elements of wet and dry have come together.

4 Tip the dough out on to a lightly floured surface and bring together with gentle care, not putting too much pressure on the dough as it is sensitive to stress. Lightly roll it out to 2.5cm thick, before cutting out your circles. As with all scones, it is advisable not to twist the cutter, as this brings them up wonky in the oven. A firm and confident slice downwards is all that is needed for well-brought-up scones.

5 Lightly sprinkle a pinch of grated Parmesan, as well as a little paprika, over each scone. Place them in the top of the oven for **15–17 minutes**, at which point they should be golden and well risen. Cream cheese, ham and cucumber work well with these. I also love chorizo, manchego and quince jelly for a more Spanish-inspired filling.

TRUST ME TIPS

• Go for it and add more cheese if you want – just withhold the water and gauge for yourself how much you need, depending on how much moisture is being provided by the extra cheese.

ORANGE AND ROSEMARY DRIZZLE CAKE

THIS CAKE IS that moment when a white-hot sunbeam inches over your cheek, and wakes you up with a smile . . . It's a lazy stroll in the waves, a world inside a book, and melon for breakfast.

SERVES 10

200g peeled **swede**, diced into 2cm cubes
2 medium free-range eggs
120g clear honey
finely grated zest of 3 oranges (juicing varieties, such as Seville, are best)
60g white rice flour
100g ground almonds
2 tsp baking powder
¼ tsp salt

FOR THE DRIZZLE

3 tbsp golden granulated sugar
125ml water
6 sprigs rosemary
4 tbsp freshly squeezed orange juice

FOR THE TOP

1 fresh sprig rosemary
1 tbsp golden granulated sugar

YOU WILL NEED

a 19cm x 12cm x 8cm (1.7 litre) loaf tin

1 Preheat the oven to 180°C/350°F/gas mark 4. Line the base of the tin with baking parchment and lightly grease the parchment and the sides of the tin with a little vegetable oil, then set aside.

2 Place the diced swede in a saucepan, cover with water and cook for 7 minutes. Once cooked through, drain off the excess water and blend to a fine purée.

3 In a large mixing bowl, whisk the eggs and honey for 2 minutes until bubbly. Add the orange zest, flour, ground almonds, baking powder and salt. Once all the ingredients are fully incorporated, whisk in the swede purée to combine.

4 Pour the mixture into the prepared tin and place in the middle of the oven for **40 minutes**.

5 Whilst the cake is cooking, make the drizzle by dissolving the sugar in the water, along with the rosemary sprigs, in a small pan. As soon as the liquid has come to the boil – by which I mean when the bubbles have crept up around the rosemary's edges and then completely engulfed the herb stalks so that you can no longer see them – take the pan off the heat. Set aside to infuse until the cake is ready.

6 Once the cake is cooked and out of the oven, prick it all over right to the bottom with a skewer so that it is covered in little holes. Leave the cake in the tin and, while it is still warm, drizzle with the sweet rosemary liquid, then pour the orange juice over.

7 Finish off by dotting a few rosemary leaves over the surface of the cake and sprinkling with the remaining tablespoon of sugar before serving.

FORBIDDEN CHOCOLATE BROWNIES

THIS RECIPE IS DANGEROUS. Sinful and completely irresistible, this brownie is so wicked that you could drown in it. Like a bad man, this is a girl's deathbed. If it were poison, you would still be glad you'd tried it.

SERVES 12

400g topped, tailed and peeled raw **beetroot**, cut into 2cm dice
100g hazelnuts
3 medium free-range eggs
220g light Muscovado sugar
¼ tsp salt
150g dark cooking chocolate (minimum 70% cocoa solids), broken into squares
2 tbsp white rice flour
70g good-quality cocoa powder
2 tsp baking powder
1 tsp vanilla extract

FOR THE TOP
30g chopped hazelnuts

YOU WILL NEED
a 27cm x 20cm x 5cm brownie tin
a blender
a microwave
a food processor

1 Preheat the oven to 160°C/325°F/gas mark 3. Line the base and sides of your tin with baking parchment. Once it is in place, lightly brush the parchment on the base and sides with a little vegetable oil.

2 Cook the diced beetroot in the microwave for 10 minutes in a heatproof bowl with a small splash of water, covered in cling film.

3 Whilst the beetroot is cooking, whizz the hazelnuts to a powder in the food processor. Take the time to grind them up as much as you can manage, even if this means blitzing in several stages.

4 Whisk the eggs, sugar and salt with a hand-held whisk in a large mixing bowl for 5 minutes until tripled in volume.

5 Next turn your attention back to the beetroot. Drain the water from the cooked, hot beetroot and blend to a purée. Add the chocolate squares before re-covering the bowl with cling film and setting aside. You need to make sure that the beetroot is piping hot or it won't melt the chocolate. If the beetroot has cooled too much, simply heat it up for 1 final minute in the microwave before proceeding with the next stage of the recipe.

6 Beat the powdered hazelnuts, flour, cocoa powder, baking powder and vanilla extract into the fluffy egg mixture until well combined.

7 Add the beetroot and melted chocolate purée to the mixture and fold through until fully incorporated.

8 Pour the mixture into the prepared tin and sprinkle the 30g chopped hazelnuts over the top. Cook in the middle of the oven for **35 minutes**.

9 Remove from the oven and cool the brownie in the tin for 20 minutes before cutting it into individual brownies and serving.

CONTINUED OVERLEAF

TRUST ME TIPS

• If the beetroot doesn't purée completely, don't worry about it but just add the chocolate. Once the chocolate has completely melted, purée again until as smooth as possible.

• Hazelnuts have a tendency to clump when being blitzed as they are very high in oil, so blitz them in two or three batches. Also, although it's great to aim for a powder, the recipe will work fine if it's a little coarser than that.

• In 'ordinary' brownie recipes, you would never expect to cook the cake for more than 20 minutes or so, to maintain the slightly raw texture. That doesn't apply to this recipe, since the beetroot furnishes the cake with squidginess and we need to cook it longer in order to set the eggs and chocolate together slightly.

• You will definitely make this recipe more than once, and you may find that you adjust the cooking time within 5 minutes or so of the 35 minutes given here. Each oven is different and you will come to know the slight variations in texture that you prefer.

• Be careful not to move this brownie too much when warm, as it is extremely delicate and will break easily until it has cooled, when it will be much easier to handle.

CAPPUCCINO CUPCAKES

THIS CUPCAKE WILL come down to dinner wearing a Chinese silk jacket if the fancy takes him. Although he's kind and smiley about the eyes, don't presume to know what he's thinking. He can be anything he wants . . . because he's magic.

MAKES 12

2 medium free-range
    eggs
160g caster sugar
200g peeled and finely
    grated **sweet
    potato**
100g white rice flour
100g ground almonds
2 tsp baking powder
¼ tsp salt
3 tbsp coffee essence
    (such as Camp; see
    page 180 for
    stockists)

FOR THE ICING

50g unsalted butter, cold
    and cubed
200g icing sugar, sieved
50g mascarpone
2 tsp coffee essence

FOR THE TOP
chocolate coffee beans

YOU WILL NEED
a 12-hole muffin tray
12 cupcake cases (see
    page xxvii for exact
    size)

1 Preheat the oven to 180°C/350°F/gas mark 4. Line the muffin tray with the paper cases.

2 Whisk the eggs and sugar in a large mixing bowl for 5 minutes, until pale and quadrupled in volume. Add the grated sweet potato and whisk again. Whisk in the flour, ground almonds, baking powder and salt, as well as the coffee essence, until they are well introduced.

3 Spoon the mixture into the cupcake cases, aiming for it to come four fifths of the way up each case. Place in the oven for **20 minutes** until the cakes are risen and cooked. Don't be alarmed that they are flat on the top rather than dome shaped.

4 Whilst the cupcakes are cooking, make the icing. Whisk the butter with an electric whisk until pale and fluffy. Next, add 100g of the icing sugar and whisk together to create a paste. Beat for an extra 10 seconds at this stage to stabilize and appease the butter.

5 Add the mascarpone and coffee essence, along with the rest of the icing sugar, and mix by hand with a wooden spoon until all are combined in a happy and unified mixture. Refrigerate until the cupcakes are ready.

6 Once cooked, remove the cakes from the oven and cool them in the tin for 15 minutes. I usually put them into the fridge to finish cooling right down so that they are cold by the time you want to ice them. Ice the cakes, using about 1 tablespoon of icing for each one. Decorate with chocolate coffee beans before serving.

TRUST ME TIPS

• Although other brands of coffee essence are available, for me Camp is the best-kept secret in the baking aisle.

CHOCOLATE AND SALTED CARAMEL SQUILLIONAIRE

THIS RECIPE IS downright spoiled. Years of getting his own way mean that this squillionaire is opinionated, pedantic and often unreasonable. Patience is required at every level, but it's worth the effort in the end . . . a squillion times over.

SERVES 12

397g tin condensed milk
100g unsalted butter, melted
3 tbsp golden syrup
300g digestive biscuits
a very small pinch of Malden sea salt
150g dark cooking chocolate (minimum 70% cocoa solids)

YOU WILL NEED

a 22cm-square x 5cm-deep brownie tin
a food processor, or a rolling pin and a heavy-duty plastic bag

1 Preheat the oven to 180°C/350°F/gas mark 4. Line the base of the tin with baking paper.

2 To make the caramel, place the tin of condensed milk in a medium saucepan. Don't use a non-stick pan, as this procedure will ruin the sensitive base. Rather use your oldest and most study pan for this job.

3 Fill the pan with boiling water until it has run over the top of the tin. Set the time for 1 hour and boil hard, topping up the water level every 10 minutes or so, as it will evaporate considerably.

4 Whilst the caramel is doing its own thing, turn your attention to the biscuit base. Put the butter and golden syrup in a heatproof dish in the oven for 5 minutes to melt. (If you first dip the tablespoon quickly into boiling water, it will make it easier to spoon the syrup out of its tin.)

5 Meanwhile crush the biscuits. You can blitz the digestives in the bowl of the food processor until you have reached a consistency like sand. If you plan on doing this with a plastic bag and a rolling pin, please be very thorough and let off some steam. Crumbs are not good enough here; we're after sand.

6 Retrieve the hot dish with the melted butter and syrup from the oven and pour it into the bowl of the food processor with your biscuit sand. Blitz briefly to mix in all the butter. Scrape the sides down with a knife and blitz again.

7 Tip the biscuit-base mixture into the prepared tin and press down with the palm of your hand, so that it is evenly distributed and quite well packed. Prick it with a fork a few times to let the air through whilst it is setting and crisping in the oven.

CONTINUED OVERLEAF

8 Place in the middle of the oven for **20 minutes** until golden and firm to the touch. Once the biscuit base is cooked, take it out of the oven and set it aside, ready for the caramel.

9 Remove the tin of condensed milk from the water after 1 hour and open it carefully, as the contents will be blisteringly hot and dying to escape from the captivity of the airtight tin. Sprinkle in the salt flakes, give it a good stir and pour the thick caramel over the biscuit base.

10 Place it in the freezer to set for 20 minutes whilst the chocolate melts. It is imperative that the caramel layer is set before pouring the chocolate over it, otherwise you will end up with a mess like a melted Mars bar.

11 Whilst the base and caramel are cooling, melt the chocolate in a bowl over boiling water until it is smooth and runny. Pour it over the caramel to make the third layer.

12 Set the cake in the fridge for another 20 minutes until cold. The chocolate will have 'bloomed' from the cold by the time it's ready to be cut and served. Run a knife around the edge before you unmould, then cut the cake into rectangles. Keeps for up to 5 days in an airtight container.

TRUST ME TIPS

• I love salted caramel, but please omit the salt if you don't like using the stuff. In any case, it really wants to be only a very, very small amount of salt in order to bring together all the wonderful flavours of caramel and chocolate.

AMERICAN VANILLA CUPCAKES

THIS IS AN LA CUPCAKE: virtually fat free, perfectly white and jogging along the beach. Its vanilla-scented body and immaculate frosting are delightfully superficial and quite without spite.

MAKES 12

2 medium free-range
    eggs
160g caster sugar
300g topped, tailed,
    peeled and finely
    grated **courgette**
180g white rice flour
2 tsp baking powder
¼ tsp salt
1 tsp vanilla extract

FOR THE ICING

1 quantity Snow
    Meringue Icing
    (see page 85)
1 vanilla pod, split
    lengthways with the
    seeds scraped out

YOU WILL NEED

a 12-hole muffin tray
12 cupcake cases (see
    page xxvii for exact
    size)

1 Preheat the oven to 180°C/350°F/gas mark 4. Arrange the paper cases neatly in the muffin tray.

2 Whisk the eggs and sugar in a large mixing bowl until pale and light – this stage takes at least 5 minutes and is achieved when the mixture leaves a ribbon-like trail when you lift the beaters. Whisk in the grated courgette briefly to incorporate.

3 Sprinkle over half the flour, along with the baking powder and salt, then whisk thoroughly for a further 20 seconds. Add the remaining flour and the vanilla extract, and whisk one final time until the mixture looks well combined.

4 Ladle the mixture into the paper cases so that it comes four fifths of the way up the sides. Place in the middle of the oven for **30 minutes**.

5 Whilst the cupcakes are quietly preening themselves in the oven, get going on making the Snow Meringue Icing (see page 85). The only amendment is that you should add the seeds from the vanilla pod to the ingredients at the beginning of the recipe before proceeding as normal.

6 Once the cupcakes are cooked, remove them from the oven and cool on a wire rack for 10 minutes. Ice when the cupcakes are cool (arguably, anyone who comes out of LA is cool, even when they come straight from the oven . . .) with the help of a round knife or small spatula.

TRUST ME TIPS

• Don't be afraid that the cake mixture is a bit runny – this is quite normal. This is a fatless sponge, which is why it will feel looser than usual sponge mixtures.

CARAMEL SWISS ROLL WITH PASSIONFRUIT CREAM

THIS CAKE HAS a delightful lisp. She always sees the funny side of things, and likes eating mango for breakfast whilst listening to Radio 4.

SERVES 8

a little icing sugar
100g topped, tailed, peeled and finely grated **carrot**
1 tsp vanilla extract
100g caster sugar
¼ tsp salt
4 medium free-range eggs, yolks and whites separated
70g white rice flour
1 tsp baking powder

FOR THE FILLING

140ml double cream
2 tbsp icing sugar, sieved
6 small passionfruit, cut in half and flesh scraped out

FOR THE CARAMEL

4 tbsp Dulce de Leche

YOU WILL NEED

a 33cm x 24cm x 2cm Swiss roll tin
a rubber spatula
a clean tea towel

1 Preheat the oven to 180°C/350°F/gas mark 4. Line the base of the Swiss roll tin with baking parchment, cutting into the corners to get a neat fit. Using a sieve, sprinkle this with icing sugar so that there is a fine layer more or less all over the base. This is important in preventing the sponge from sticking to the bottom.

2 Weigh out the grated carrot on a plate and pour over the vanilla extract. Weigh out the flour and baking powder on to another plate.

3 Measure the caster sugar into a small mixing bowl with the salt. Now remove 2 tbsp of the sugar and put them into a large mixing bowl with the egg whites. Whisk until the egg whites are stiff. Set the large mixing bowl aside.

4 Add the egg yolks to the sugar in the smaller mixing bowl and whisk for a full 4 minutes until they are pale, fluffy and hold a ribbon trail when you lift the beaters. Add the carrot, flour and baking powder to the egg-yolk mixture and whisk to combine.

5 With the help of a rubber spatula, beat one third of the egg whites into the egg-yolk mixture. And when I say 'beat', I mean roll up your sleeves and give it a good mix.

6 Taking care to work delicately and quickly so as not to knock out too much of the air, cautiously fold in the next third of egg whites. To do this, spoon the egg white into the middle of the bowl, so that it is sitting on the bubbly mixture, then go under the contents of the bowl with your spatula as if you were cleaning the sides, and dump the liquid from the bottom on to the floating egg-white island in the middle of the bowl. Then, decisively cut through the middle of the floating egg white with the side of your spatula and repeat the process until it has broken up and blended in an airy pillow with the heavier liquid part. Repeat the process with the final third of egg white.

7 Pour the mixture carefully into the prepared Swiss roll tin, aiming to drag the lazy mixture from the bowl into the centre of the tin. This makes it easier to tilt the tin this way and that to coax the mixture into the corners of the tin, so that it doesn't just lie in the

CONTINUED OVERLEAF

centre. Don't pat it down with the spatula, as this will knock out the air completely. It is important for the mixture to reach all corners of the tin, since the mixture will set and start to cook very soon after it has gone into the oven because it is so flat and exposed. How it goes into the tin is how it will end up looking once cooked.

8 Cook in the middle of the oven for **20 minutes**.

9 Once cooked, it is important to act quickly. Lay a clean tea towel flat on an empty kitchen surface and cover it with a slightly smaller rectangle of baking parchment of the same shape. Take the tray out of the oven and carefully lift the sponge out of its tin, holding it with the edges of the baking parchment. Don't be frightened by the sponge that is clinging to the paper; it is quite safe and much more robust than you think.

10 Lay the sponge, exposed side down, on to the baking parchment in the middle of the tea towel (lay it out lengthways so that it looks like two rectangles that fit into each other) and carefully peel off the paper from the back of the cooked sponge, which will come off easily in your hands.

11 The next stage is the most important of all. Start from one end of the cloth and roll a cigar shape with the tea towel and baking parchment. When you come to the sponge, continue to roll it snugly, so that the sponge and the towel are meshed together in a roly-poly shape. Continue until all the sponge is cosily tucked up inside the tea towel. Let it stand for 10 minutes to cool and semi-set in a snail shape whilst you make the passionfruit cream filling.

12 Sieve the icing sugar into the cream and beat for 1 minute until stiff. As always, don't over-whip the cream or it will go grainy and split and splutter. Gently fold in the flesh from the passionfruit to create a rippled effect. Keep in the fridge until needed.

13 Once the sponge has had 10 minutes to cool off and slightly set, unroll it from its paper and tea towel, and spread a generous layer of warm Dulce de Leche all over the inside. Remove the cream from the fridge and spread it over the top of the caramel layer.

14 Roll the bulging sponge up again and don't worry about the mess. It's bound to crack a little here and overspill a little there. Sieve over 2 tbsp icing sugar and refrigerate until needed. Take the Swiss roll out 10 minutes before serving for a lighter result.

TRUST ME TIPS

• By all means use whipping cream instead of double if you want to slash the naughty factor – it's not got quite the same clout, but the sponge is light and moist enough to take a low-fat centre. The sponge itself is so delicious that I often just make it with the passionfruit cream centre and do away with the caramel altogether, which of course removes most of the fat and sugar from the recipe.

• I have recently discovered the dangerous Confiture de Caramel from Bonne Maman, which you could use to replace the Dulce de Leche.

• Don't worry about handling the sponge at the rolling and unrolling stages. There is plenty of natural spring and bounce in the sponge, which means that it will easily cope with a bit of rough handling.

MINT CHOC CHIP CUPCAKES

THIS CUPCAKE IS seriously bossy and much more 'Peppermint' than 'Mint'. If only she had had the foresight to keep her full title when she was at school. 'Mint' is very familiar (and 'Minty' is even worse) . . . She's an icon of the eighties, and is wearing a green feather in her hair to make sure that people notice her.

MAKES 12

2 medium free-range eggs
160g caster sugar
200g topped, tailed, peeled and finely grated **courgette**
90g white rice flour
100g ground almonds
2 tsp good-quality cocoa powder
1 tsp peppermint extract
2 tsp baking powder
¼ tsp salt
100g mint-flavoured dark chocolate, or plain dark (minimum 70% cocoa solids), chopped into chunks

FOR THE ICING

50g unsalted butter, softened
200g icing sugar, sieved
50g mascarpone
2 tsp good-quality cocoa powder
½ tsp peppermint extract

FOR THE TOP

a dozen small fresh mint leaves

YOU WILL NEED

a 12-hole muffin tray
12 cupcake cases (see page xxvii for exact size)

1 Preheat the oven to 180°C/350°F/gas mark 4. Line the muffin tray with paper cases.

2 Whisk the eggs and sugar in a large mixing bowl for 5 minutes, until pale and quadrupled in volume. Add the grated courgette and whisk again. Whisk in the flour, ground almonds, cocoa powder, peppermint extract, baking powder and salt until they are well introduced. Finally, add the chocolate chunks and mix them in with a spatula so that they are dotted evenly around the place.

3 Ladle the mixture evenly between the cupcake cases in the tin so that it comes four fifths of the way up the side of the cases.

4 Place the cakes in the oven for **20 minutes** until risen and cooked. Don't be alarmed that they are flat on the top rather than dome shaped.

5 Whilst the cupcakes are cooking, make the icing. Whisk the butter with an electric whisk until pale and fluffy. Next, add 100g of the sugar and whisk to create a lovely rich paste.

6 Add the mascarpone, the cocoa powder and peppermint extract, as well as the remaining icing sugar. Beat by hand using a wooden spoon to combine. Refrigerate for at least 15 minutes.

7 Once the cupcakes are cooked, remove them from the oven and cool in the tin for 15 minutes. I usually put them into the fridge after this to finish cooling right down so that they are cold by the time I want to ice them. To ice, use roughly 1 tbsp of icing per cupcake. Top each one with a small mint leaf before serving.

CONTINUED OVERLEAF

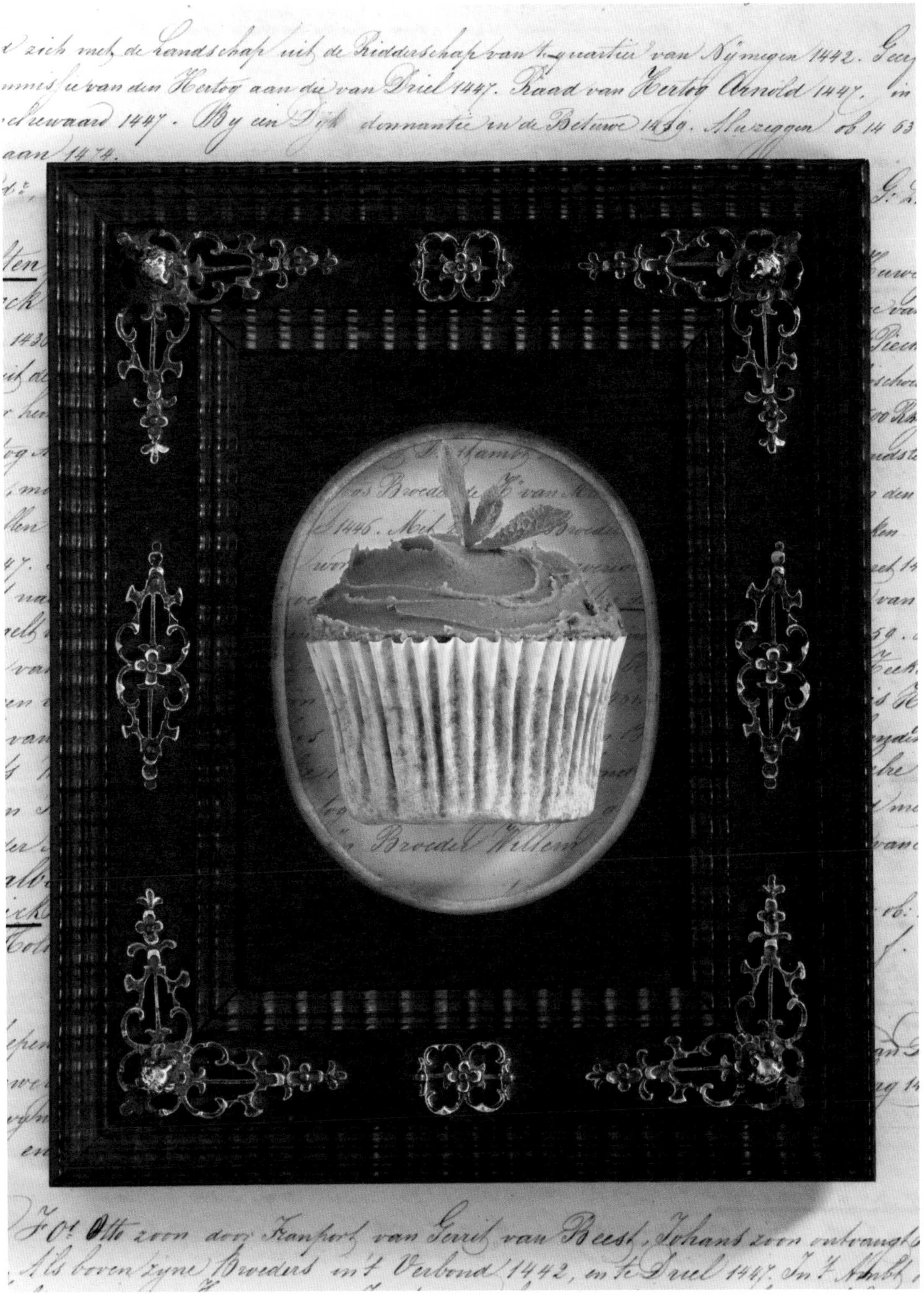

TRUST ME TIPS

- Beware of fiddling with the amounts of peppermint extract – it is as delicious when used in the correct amounts as it is a headache when abused.

- It should be easy enough to get hold of peppermint extract (essence isn't as good) at a good supermarket.

- Don't be alarmed that the mixture is rather runny when it comes to spooning it into the paper cases – that's just the way it is (mine is like that too).

- Cooling in the tin is not just a whimsical instruction on my part. The cupcakes are deliberately a tiny bit under-cooked when they come out of the oven and need to finish off super-gently in the tin, so that the chocolate chips keep some shape and the cupcake doesn't dry out.

Cake Diaries

RED VELVET CAKE

Testing Number 1: 13 March
Very dense, very red and frankly not nice but a damn sight more like cake than that obtuse and obscene coffee and hazelnut disaster. So there is hope.

Testing Number 2: 13 March
Got thoroughly over-excited watching her through the oven door as she heaved effortlessly in her three tins. When I put the cocoa powder in, I got a little worried as I couldn't remember if it was a teaspoon or a tablespoon . . . and sure enough it's too brown. Rats, rats, and more rats – especially since the fluff and flavour were just awesome. Not altogether thrilled with the icing, I have to admit.

Testing Number 3: 14 March
This I took to the Shorts' who liked it overall. John Short thought the beetroot flavour too intense and frankly, I agree. I got a bit panicky about this. The colour is flipping fantastic though and the texture is good.

Testing Number 4: 14 March
Changed the icing, downed the beetroot again and hoped for the best . . . Significantly better flavour than the last one. Amazing to consider what a huge difference 100g of beetroot has made – quite stunning. Still, the colour is definitely not *quite* right and the icing isn't perfect. I may have to go back to the drawing board on this one. I'm going to have to set her aside for today as I need a change of mindset lest I start to resent her.

Testing Number One Billion (OK, only 5): 22nd April
I can't believe it's only testing number five – I feel like I've been trying to tweak this little tease on and off for the last seven months (maybe more in my mind than in real life). The outcome is still not quite right. The colour is not red enough. It's the liquid dye, which isn't working at all. Otherwise the texture is good. Maybe bring back the buttermilk?

Testing Number 6: 21 October
I was sitting in bed this morning thinking that Red Velvet could do with a serious injection of ground almonds to give her some more height, some uniformity, and some pride mostly.

Testing Number 7: 22nd April
I haven't tasted it yet, but looking at her makes me so excited I could giggle . . . she looks perfect. My only fleeting thought is 'Should I risk an extra teaspoon of cocoa if the flavour needs it, as I don't want to ruin the colour?' Anyway, for now, get making some snow, girl . . . Well. Nothing is absolutely perfect. I've gone and blown the Snow Meringue Icing (all 16 minutes of beating) by adding silly old cream cheese. As for the cake itself, I want to test it again with that extra cocoa and lose the vanilla (which is undetectable). Yes to buttermilk and paste dye! Excellent texture. Also, the cake is not too sweet which is important in view of the icing.

Testing Number 8: 14 November
Wow. She's making me work for it . . .
I'm surprised at myself because in some
twisted way, I am growing to respect her
for being such a difficult girl to pin down!
She's good . . .

Testing Number 9: 4 December
It's another turn on the Red Velvet merry-
go-round. This 'grande dame' wants to go
out in spectacular fashion, I see . . . Well,
why not – I'm resigned to her now, and
have accepted that things must be on her
terms or not at all.

Testing Number 10: 4 December
I was really rather nervous on this testing as
I *so* wish her to come out just right. So far
one observation is screamingly obvious: the
icing needs to be tried using icing sugar.
OK, OK, OK, I'm so close. This is
electrifying. One more time should
definitely do it.

Testing Number 11: 8 December
Apparently it's only number eleven, yet I
feel that I have been coaxing this madam
into behaving since before my birth. I'd
better speak quietly as she's in the oven
right now and might overhear me. I'm
ready for rejection but my heart will swell
with relief if today is the day. It's the
flavour that I'm particularly keen to chase
down – more fluff, less sourness . . . I feel a
bit like crying because I've got here in the
end. My hands are all stained with beetroot
and dye but my heart is full of joy. At long
last. Thank you, Red Velvet. What a trip
this has been.

ORANGE AND ROSEMARY DRIZZLE CAKE

Testing Number 1: 20 December
This book never ceases to amaze and delight
me – at number seventy-six I have just
turned out the most exquisite orange and
rosemary drizzle . . . A wonderful balance of
clumsy, wet texture and a light crumb that is
slightly shy.

FORBIDDEN CHOCOLATE BROWNIES

Testing Number 1: 14 September
This one went into the oven tasting
awesome – and smells amazing now. It's
curious how those hazelnuts refuse to
powder; it's like they stick together for dear
life and only ever get to 'chunky dust'
stage. Let's down the nuts by 50g, up the
beetroot by 100g, up the sugar by 50g (and
switch to soft brown). Nevertheless, this is
unbelievable. The depth of the chocolate
flavour is insane; it's like a bottomless
chocolate pit. I don't think that I have ever
written such a chocolate chocolate recipe
. . . Wow. I'm going to try a second
version with these amendments just to be
sure in my heart that it's the best that it can
be, but it's pretty amazing right now.
Blows your head off.

Testing Number 2: 14 April
A couple of minor amendments and I think
that although it's still a bit squidgy, it's a
triumph (and half the fun is that it just feels
bad). It's completely irresistible.

CHOCOLATE AND SALTED CARAMEL SQUILLIONAIRE

Testing Number 1: 2 October
This is wrong on two out of three levels (chocolate being the only one to respond). Oh goodness, how depressing. It's that familiar sinking feeling again . . . The base is wrong – this does not want to be a flapjack. Granny is right – it wants to be a biscuit (one of my favourite words). And all that palaver last week should have taught me not to meddle with fudge for the middle – far too capricious.

Testing Number 2: 3 October
Wow, this cantankerous recipe is a whisker off being sent to the graveyard . . .

Testing Number 3: 8 October
God, this one's hard work – and selfish! Not quite right. I'm now cross with him. I'm going to nail this one even if it kills me. Grrr.

Testing Number 4: 9 October
Now come on, you brat. Deep breath. Still not quite there yet.

Testing Number 5: 18 October
Only the base to sort – and I sincerely hope that this is the one. It's by far the best-looking mixture to go into the tin so there's hope . . . The base is still not right! I could scream and jump up and down with frustration! Digestive biscuits are the last possible solution before I resolutely put this exasperating recipe into the graveyard.

Testing Number 6: 20 October
OK. Well, the base is crunchy and blonde . . . and made with digestive biscuits, golden syrup and butter! There's no vegetable left in but I still want to keep him. *How* did he manage it?

AMERICAN VANILLA CUPCAKES

Testing Number 1: 22 September
I'm trying my luck with a bit more courgette (300g all in) as opposed to 250g. Fingers crossed this should be a bit of an ally . . . To say that they are perfect is an understatement; they're a dream. Delightful bimbos without a bad bone in their body.

CHOCOLATE
HEARTACHE

HEARTACHE CHOCOLATE CAKE

THIS CAKE IS SAD. It's dark and drizzling down the window panes. She puffs her chest in hope when she goes into the oven; she then breaks, like a chest heaving a sob. This is why Aubergine (the Eeyore of the vegetable world) is the right kind of friend to hold your hand.

SERVES 14

2 small whole
    aubergines
    (weighing roughly
    400g)
300g best dark
    chocolate you can
    find (minimum
    70% cocoa solids
    essential), broken
    into squares
50g good-quality cocoa
    powder, plus extra
    for dusting
60g ground almonds
3 medium free-range
    eggs
200g clear honey
2 tsp baking powder
¼ tsp salt (or some tears,
    if you have them in
    the kitchen)
1 tbsp brandy (for moral
    support)

YOU WILL NEED

a 23cm-diameter x
    7cm-deep loose-
    bottomed tin
a skewer
a microwave
a blender

1 Preheat the oven to 180°C/350°F/gas mark 4. Line the tin with baking parchment and lightly brush the base and sides with a little oil.

2 Cook the aubergines by puncturing their skins erratically here and there with a skewer, then placing them in a bowl covered with cling film. Microwave on high for 8 minutes until the vegetables are cooked and limp. Discard any water at the bottom. Leave the aubergines to stand in the bowl until they are cool enough to handle.

3 Next, skin (I find that the tip of a knife does the job) and purée the aubergines in the blender. Once the warm aubergine is puréed and smooth, add the chocolate, which will mingle and melt slowly. Set aside, covered once again in cling film, until all the chocolate has melted.

4 In a large bowl, whisk up all the other ingredients for a minute until well introduced to each other and slightly tipsy (bubbly). Fold the melted chocolate and aubergine mixture into the bowl with all the other ingredients. Don't be afraid of being a little brutal with the spatula – they will get on and fuse.

5 Pour the mixture into the prepared tin and place it in the bottom of the oven for **30 minutes**, by which time your kitchen will just sing with the smell of hot chocolate.

6 Remove the cake from the oven and let it cool in its tin for 15 minutes before turning it out on to a wire rack and peeling off the parchment. Quickly turn it the right way up again and sit it on a plate to avoid any scars from the rack.

7 Sieve a little cocoa powder over the top of the cake before cutting yourself a slice and letting the medicine work its magic.

CONTINUED OVERLEAF

157

- If you don't have a microwave, peel and cube the aubergines and cook them with a tiny splash of water on top of the hob until they are soft and squidgy, taking great care neither to burn them nor to drown them with too much water. Discard the water before blitzing.

- Make sure that the aubergine has definitely melted the chocolate – this is not an instance where chunks of chocolate are wanted, I'm afraid. If the aubergine is too cool, simply blitz it in the microwave for another 2 minutes before adding the chocolate chunks.

- Be very careful to unmould the cake when it is cool rather than warm – it is terribly delicate (just as you are) and could smash easily. A little time to cool down helps make it more robust.

- On particularly sad days, this cake will crack on the surface when it's cooking. Don't be upset by this – it's just the heart of the cake breaking too and trying to make you feel less alone.

CHOCOLATE AND CHESTNUT ROULADE

THIS ROULADE IS a diplomatic, whiskerish old man. Now that he's retired, he has time to think about important things like trees. Contrary to what 'the young' think, there's only one way to build a fire, and anyone who's been in the Army knows that.

SERVES 8

a little icing sugar
100g caster sugar
¼ tsp salt
4 medium free-range
    eggs, yolks and
    whites separated
3 tbsp good-quality
    cocoa powder
100g peeled and finely
    grated **sweet
    potato**
60g white rice flour
1 tsp baking powder

FOR THE FILLING

140ml double cream
2 tbsp icing sugar, sieved
1 tsp vanilla extract
200g sweet chestnut
    purée (see page
    180 for stockists)

FOR THE TOP

2 tbsp good-quality
    cocoa powder

YOU WILL NEED

a 33cm x 24cm x 2cm
    Swiss roll tin
a rubber spatula
a clean tea towel

1 Preheat the oven to 180°C/350°F/gas mark 4 and line the base of the Swiss roll tin with baking parchment, cutting into the corners to get a neat fit. Using a sieve, sprinkle the parchment with icing sugar so that there is a fine layer more or less all over the base. This is important in helping prevent the sponge from sticking to the bottom.

2 Weigh out the grated sweet potato on to a plate. Weigh out the flour and baking powder on to another plate.

3 Measure the caster sugar into a small mixing bowl with the salt. Now remove 2 tbsp of the sugar and place them in a large mixing bowl with the egg whites. Whisk until the egg whites are stiff. Set the large mixing bowl aside.

4 Whisk the sugar and egg yolks in the smaller mixing bowl for a full 4 minutes until they are pale, fluffy and hold a ribbon trail when you lift the beaters. Add the cocoa powder to the egg-yolk mixture, one tablespoon at a time, whisking well between additions. Once you have a thickish chocolate-coloured paste, add the sweet potato and whisk to incorporate.

5 With the help of a rubber spatula, beat one third of the egg whites into the chocolate egg-yolk mixture. You can be quite brutal here, as it's only a brash introduction of one element to another. You're ploughing the field for the diplomatic step, which comes next.

6 Taking care to work delicately and quickly so as not to knock out too much of the air, cautiously fold in the next third of egg whites. To do this, spoon the egg white into the middle of the bowl, so that it is sitting on the bubbly chocolate mixture, then go under the contents of the bowl with your spatula as if you were cleaning the sides, and dump the liquid from the bottom on to the floating egg-white island in the middle of the bowl. Then decisively cut through the middle of the floating egg white with the side of your spatula and repeat the process until it has broken up and blended in an airy pillow with the heavier liquid part.

CONTINUED OVERLEAF

7 Repeat the process with the final third of the egg white and at the same time sieve the flour and baking powder into the mixture. Fold as before until all elements are incorporated.

8 Pour the mixture carefully into the prepared Swiss roll tin, aiming to drag the lazy mixture from the bowl into the centre of the tin. This makes it easier to tilt the tin this way and that to coax the mixture into the corners of the tin, so that it doesn't just lie in the centre. Don't pat it down with the spatula, as this will knock out the air completely. It is important for the mixture to reach all corners of the tin, since the mixture will set and start to cook very soon after it has gone into the oven because it is so exposed. How it goes into the tin is how it will end up looking once cooked. Cook in the middle of the oven for **15 minutes**.

9 Once cooked, it is important to act quickly. Lay a clean tea towel flat on an empty kitchen surface and cover it with a slightly smaller rectangle of baking parchment of the same shape. Take the tray out of the oven and carefully lift the sponge out of its tin, holding it with the edges of the baking parchment. Don't be frightened by the sponge that is clinging to the paper; it is quite safe and much more robust than you think.

10 Place the sponge, exposed side down, on the baking parchment in the middle of the tea towel (lay it out lengthways so that it looks like two rectangles that fit into each other) and carefully peel off the baking parchment from the back of the cooked sponge; it will come off easily in your hands.

11 The next stage is the most important of all. Start from one end of the cloth and roll a cigar shape with the tea towel and baking parchment. When you come to the sponge, continue to roll it snugly, so that the sponge and the towel are rolled up together in a roly-poly shape. Continue until all the sponge is cosily tucked up inside the tea towel. Let it stand for 10 minutes to cool and semi-set in a snail shape whilst you make the chestnut cream filling.

12 Beat the cream with the icing sugar and vanilla extract for 1 minute until stiff. As always, don't over-whip the cream, or it will go grainy and split and splutter. Cover and put it away in the fridge until needed.

13 Once the sponge has had 10 minutes to cool off and slightly set, unroll it from its paper and tea towel, and spread a generous layer of chestnut purée all over the inside. Remove the cream from the fridge and spread it over the top of the purée layer. Grate the chocolate (if using) evenly on top of the cream.

14 Roll the bulging sponge up again and don't worry about the mess. It's bound to crack a little here and over-spill a little there. Sieve about 2 tbsp cocoa powder over the roulade and refrigerate until needed. Take it out 10 minutes before serving for a lighter result.

TRUST ME TIPS

• There are at least two sorts of sweetened chestnut purée on the market in Britain. The one that I particularly like to use also contains vanilla and the list of stockists on page 180 should help you find it. Other versions are fine for the purpose of this recipe, but are not delicious enough for you to want to eat with a spoon out of the jar.

• Don't hesitate to change the cream and filling to whatever takes your fancy. I find it wickedly delicious to spread Nutella over the sponge instead of chestnut purée, and to add a handful of chopped hazelnuts to the cream filling. If you would prefer a lower-fat filling, you can use whipping cream instead of double.

• As for a bit of rough handling during the rolling part of the sponge – don't worry about cracking or damaging it. As long as you treat it with confidence, no harm will come to it. In fact you might be surprised at how much bounce is contained in this sponge!

PEAR AND PECAN CALVADOS CAKE

A FINE MIST OF DRIZZLE covers the window frame and the backdrop of the trees beyond. Pear and Pecan Calvados Cake is laid out on the desk in the bay window, as if waiting for the spell to pass. Still and patient, this recipe is a quiet story of silent words.

SERVES 12

3 small firm pears, such
    as Conference
    (whole weight
    300g)
½ lemon
150g pecans
150g white rice flour
2 tsp baking powder
¼ tsp salt
1 vanilla pod, split
    lengthways and
    seeds scraped out
2 tsp ground ginger
1 tsp cinnamon
3 medium free-range
    eggs
180g caster sugar
200g topped, tailed,
    peeled and super-
    finely grated
    parsnip
125ml Calvados

FOR THE TOP
icing sugar

YOU WILL NEED
a 23cm-diameter x
    7cm-deep loose-
    bottomed tin
a food processor
kitchen string

1 Preheat the oven to 200°C/400°F/gas mark 6. Lightly brush the base and sides of the tin with a little vegetable oil.

2 Cut out two circles of baking parchment the same size as the base of the tin. Also cut one circle of tin foil slightly larger than the diameter of the tin.

3 Then take a sheet of baking parchment roughly 75cm long. Fold the long stretch of parchment over itself three times. Snip along the folded edge at 2cm intervals; the cuts should also measure roughly 2cm. Line the sides of the tin with this parchment, with the cut edge at the bottom, so that the little snipped bits fold into the centre of the tin. You may need to use your fingers to bend them into obedience.

4 Once all the little tags are facing the centre, place the first circle of baking parchment on the base of the tin, then lightly brush it and the paper around the side with a little oil. Finally, place the second circle of parchment over the first, and brush this one with oil too. Set the lined tin aside until needed.

5 Peel, core and thinly slice the pears. Pop them on to a medium-sized plate and squeeze the juice of the half lemon over them with your hand. Give them a quick toss to make sure that they are all coated before setting aside.

6 Whizz the pecans in the bowl of the food processor until really well ground. This will take a couple of minutes of pulsing. Add the flour, baking powder, salt, vanilla seeds, ground ginger and cinnamon to the bowl, and whizz for a full minute to combine and grind the pecans further still. Set aside.

7 In a large mixing bowl, whisk together the eggs and sugar until pale and tripled in volume (this takes roughly 3 minutes on 'full speed ahead'). Add the grated parsnip to the egg mixture.

8 Next add the dry ingredients and give a thoroughly good mix, so that nobody in the bowl is left out. Pour the Calvados over the mixture, and whizz briefly again to loosen it.

9 Pour half the mixture into the bottom of the tin and cover with half the pear slices. Try to avoid the slices overlapping in order to keep the cake as light as possible. Pour in the rest of the cake mixture. Finally, add the other half of the pear slices in a pretty round flower pattern on the top.

10 Place the foil circle over the tin, making sure that it is not touching the surface of the cake. Gently crinkle the foil paper over the edge of the tin to secure it. Tie a piece of string round the tin over the foil to make sure that the foil doesn't let in the sun and tan the cake in the hot oven.

11 Bake on a wire rack in the bottom of the oven for **2 hours**, without peeping. Once cooked, remove from the oven and brush the pear slices on the top with a little water. Be careful not to wet the cake around the slices. Sieve a generous sprinkling of icing sugar over the lot. Serve either cold with warm Crème Anglaise flavoured with 12 scratches of nutmeg (see pages 50–1), or warm with Crème au Calvados (see page 20).

TRUST ME TIPS

• Avoid grating the parsnip too far in advance, as it will go brown within about 5 minutes.

• This cake is not suitable for freezing, and is best eaten warm, straight from the oven.

PISTACHIO POPS

THIS LITTLE CAKE is called Pop because she's tiny. She's fizzing around the party in a pair of stylish green kitten heels.

MAKES 24

50g pistachios
1 medium free-range egg
50g caster sugar
100g topped, tailed,
    washed and finely
    grated **courgette**
35g white rice flour
1 tsp baking powder
small pinch of salt
a little green food
    colouring paste
    (see page 180
    for stockists)

FOR THE ICING
125g icing sugar, sieved
1 tbsp water, plus a
    further 1 tsp water
1 tsp vanilla extract
green food colouring
    paste

FOR THE TOP
24 pistachios

YOU WILL NEED
two 12-hole baby
    muffin trays
24 baby cupcake cases
    (see page xxvii for
    exact size)

1 Preheat the oven to 160°C/325°F/gas mark 3. Line your muffin trays with the paper cases.

2 Whizz the pistachios in the food processor for a couple of minutes to grind them into a powder. Scrape down the sides with a knife and whizz again. Set aside on a plate.

3 Whisk together the egg and sugar in a large mixing bowl until fluffy and pale – this should take no more than a couple of minutes. Add the grated courgette, and beat again until fully incorporated. Finally, add the pistachio dust, flour, baking powder and salt to the mixture. Give one final whisk for a minute or so, to make sure that everyone inside the bowl is on the same page. Add the most microscopic amount of green colouring with the end of a toothpick and stir to mix thoroughly.

4 With the help of two teaspoons, carefully plop a small dollop of the mixture into each case, making sure to leave a little space (say 1cm) at the top. The idea is to end up with delicate little drops, rather than loud and noisy exclamations that are popping out of their shirts!

5 Bake the cakes in the oven for **15 minutes**, then take them out and cool them on a wire rack whilst you prepare the icing.

6 To make the icing, simply combine the icing sugar, tablespoon of water and the vanilla extract with a fork or sauce whisk until smooth. Run a little colouring paste through it with a toothpick until you arrive at a nutty shade of green. Beware: a tiny amount of colour goes a very long way . . . If you are using the icing at a much later stage, place a sheet of cling film directly on to the surface to prevent it from forming a skin.

7 When the Pops are cooled, ice them individually with a teaspoon. Finally, add a whole pistachio to the top of each Pop and off you go!

Pistachio Pops, Chocolate Full Stops, White Rabbits

CHOCOLATE FULL STOPS

THESE LITTLE MOUTHFULS are well brought up: they are wonderfully cooperative, take almost no time either to prepare or cook, and gently put the lid on dinner like a miniature chocolate bullet.

MAKES 24

150g peeled **butternut squash**, cut into 1cm cubes

50g dark chocolate (minimum 70% cocoa solids), broken into squares

1 medium free-range egg

60g caster sugar

20g white rice flour

20g ground almonds

20g good-quality cocoa powder

2 tsp baking powder

small pinch of salt

FOR THE ICING

100g golden icing sugar, sieved

20g good-quality cocoa powder, sieved

2 tbsp strong black coffee (or boiling water if you don't like coffee)

FOR THE TOP

small silver or gold balls

YOU WILL NEED

two 12-hole baby muffin trays

24 baby cupcake cases (see page xxvii for exact size)

a blender

1 Preheat the oven to 180°C/350°F/gas mark 4. Line the muffin trays with the paper cases.

2 Put the cubed butternut squash into a saucepan and cover with water. Boil for 6 minutes until cooked through. Discard the water and add the pieces of chocolate. Let them stand for 2 minutes until the chocolate is completely melted.

3 Whisk the eggs and sugar in a large mixing bowl for a full 3 minutes until thick and full of air. Add the flour, ground almonds, cocoa powder, baking powder and salt to the mixing bowl. Whisk until everything is well mixed together.

4 Blend the chocolate and butternut squash mixture together until you get a smooth purée. Finally, whisk the purée into the egg mixture until combined.

5 With the help of two teaspoons, dollop one teaspoon of mixture into each little case so that it comes four fifths of the way up the side. Bake in the oven for **12 minutes**.

6 Once cooked, remove the cakes from the oven and set them to cool on a wire rack while you start on the icing.

7 Mix the icing sugar and cocoa powder in a small mixing bowl, add the first tablespoon of coffee or boiling water and, using the back of a wooden spoon, work into a smooth paste. Add the other tablespoons of liquid, one at a time with a bit of mixing in between. If you are not using the icing until much later, place a sheet of cling film directly on the surface to prevent it forming a skin.

8 Ice each Full Stop with a little of the icing on the back of a teaspoon, giving them a little pool of gloss on their tops. Finish them off with a gold or silver ball for decoration.

WHITE RABBITS

THESE LITTLE CAKES are like wisps of cloud charging across the sky, or like thoughts racing through the mind. They are not the kind of cakes that sit plump, puffed up and pleased, waiting for tea to appear. They behave a little like the White Rabbit in *Alice in Wonderland*, who is always so late for everything that he scatters anxious thoughts like petals of confetti.

MAKES 24

1 medium free-range egg
50g caster sugar
100g topped, tailed, peeled and finely grated **courgette**
1 tsp almond extract
25g white rice flour
60g ground almonds
1 tsp baking powder
small pinch of salt (optional)

FOR THE ICING

125g icing sugar, sieved
1 tbsp water
1 tsp vanilla extract
1 tsp almond extract

FOR THE TOP

little white flowers or sugar puffs (to look like tails)

YOU WILL NEED

two 12-hole baby muffin trays
24 baby cupcake cases (see page xxvii for exact size)

1 Preheat the oven to 160°C/325°F/gas mark 3. Line your muffin trays with the paper cases.

2 Whisk together the egg and sugar in a large mixing bowl, until as fluffy and pale as a bunny tail – this should take no more than a couple of minutes. Add the grated courgette and almond extract, and beat again until fully incorporated. Finally, add the flour, ground almonds, baking powder and salt (if using) to the mixture. Give one final whisk for a minute or so, to make sure that everyone inside the bowl is on the same page.

3 With the help of two teaspoons, carefully plop a small dollop of the mixture into each case, making sure to leave a little space (say half a centimetre) at the top. The idea is to end up with delicate little drops, rather than loud and noisy exclamations that are popping out of their shirts!

4 Bake the cakes in the oven for **15 minutes**, then take them out and cool them on a wire rack whilst you prepare the icing.

5 To make the icing, simply combine the icing sugar, water, vanilla and almond extract with a fork or sauce whisk until smooth. If using at a much later stage, place a sheet of cling film directly on the surface of the icing to prevent it from forming a skin.

6 Ice the Rabbits individually with a teaspoon. Finally, add your little white tails and hop along . . .

Parsnip Vanilla Fudge

THIS RECIPE IS FULL OF MISCHIEF and requires constant attention, plenty of patience and a strong arm. Imagine how tired you might be if you spent an hour with Willy Wonka and you've probably got a good idea of what's involved here.

SERVES 25

200g peeled and cubed
    parsnip
450g caster sugar
30g unsalted butter
335g condensed milk
½ tsp salt
1 vanilla pod, split
    lengthways with a
    knife and seeds
    scraped out

YOU WILL NEED

a 22cm-square x 5cm-
    deep brownie tin
a blender
a heatproof rubber
    spatula
a timer
an hour of peace and
    quiet

1 Cover the base of the tin with baking parchment. Grease the parchment lightly.

2 Place the cubed parsnip into a medium-sized saucepan and cover with water. Boil for 8 minutes until the parsnips are totally cooked through. Discard the water before whizzing to a purée. This purée needs to be very fine in order to prevent the fudge being lumpy, so please be particular about this. You should aim for a result similar to waxy mashed potato.

3 Put all the ingredients, including the parsnip purée, into a small (non-stick is easiest) saucepan over a low heat and stir with the spatula so that the condensed milk and sugar are well combined. Warm gently on the lowest possible heat until the sugar has completely dissolved and there are no gritty sand grains at the bottom or on the sides of the pan at all. This process can take up to 15 minutes and it's no good trying to rush it. It's a good idea to stir at 1- or 2-minute intervals, just to make sure that the butter is melting and that everything is mixed in well. This stage is crucial to the success of the recipe and must be given the time it needs to get there. Behaving aggressively with the mixture and forcing it into a premature boil will crystallize it – this is a pretty word for very ugly, bad-tempered, tantrum fudge.

4 Once all the sugar grains have dissolved, turn up the heat a fraction (and I really do mean the minutest amount) and get ready to stir gently for the next 25 minutes exactly (a timer is a really good idea here).

5 Make sure that you move your spatula continually over the entire base of the pan as well as into the corners in a patient but thorough motion. You can expect to hear a slight sizzle, which is where the sugar mixture has marginally overheated; it is perfectly healthy. If, on the other hand, you hear a big hiss (the likes of which you might expect from tugging hard on the tail of a cat), it's definitely time to turn down the heat and be ashamed of your hastiness.

CONTINUED OVERLEAF

6 The sorts of sounds you should expect to hear when making fudge include: a soft thud from the large bubbles bursting lethargically at the surface, and the distant hissing song of the lazy fudge on the bottom of the pan when your spatula turns it in its sleep.

7 The contents in the pan will gradually get more suntanned and you will know that you have arrived at your destination (in the glass elevator) when you reach a blonde butterscotch colour after the time is up. The texture at this point should be thick but not heavy.

8 At this stage, remove the fudge from the heat and beat it for 3 minutes exactly, which will thicken the fudge and start to set it. If you find that it is becoming too heavy before the whole 3 minutes are up, stop beating – this means that it is ready.

9 Pour the fudge carefully into the prepared tin. It will be setting very fast at this stage, so it's a good idea to have a palette knife to hand as well as the spatula. Pat the surface of the fudge down with the rubber end of the spatula to smooth over the top. Set it aside for at least an hour to cool. Cut into 5cm squares and serve, or store in an airtight container for up to 2 weeks.

TRUST ME TIPS

• The correct spatula is rather important in this recipe – I mean by that one that is flexible and doesn't keep on losing its head in the mixture (if you get my drift) but is able to remain sanguine, reliable, and attached throughout.

• Although this recipe is pretty high on the naughty stakes, you can glow with virtue in the knowledge that it will also get you on the road to Baywatch Biceps . . . I'm not joking when I say that a serious physical effort is required when it comes to 15 minutes of combined stirring and beating. It's up to you but I normally take off my jumper and tune into the radio, ready for the workout. If you have a small trouble that you want to think through or if you are particularly cross, this part of the recipe is a great way to let off steam.

Sweet Potato and Caraway Scones

THESE LITTLE FELLAS are solid citizens. They work well with clotted cream and jam (strawberry or apricot are my favourites), as well as savoury flavours like cheese and chicory. They're jolly useful to have about the place, and willing to help with the washing-up.

MAKES 10

250g white spelt flour, plus a little extra for rolling and dusting
2 tsp baking powder
½ tsp bicarbonate of soda
½ tsp salt
40g unsalted butter, cold and cubed
200g peeled and super-finely grated **sweet potato**
1 tbsp clear honey
1 tbsp caraway seeds

YOU WILL NEED

a 6cm pastry-cutter
a food processor

1 Preheat the oven to 200°C/400°F/gas mark 6. Line a baking sheet with foil and baking parchment. Lightly brush the parchment with a little oil.

2 Put the flour, baking powder, bicarbonate of soda, salt and butter into the bowl of the food processor and blitz for 10 seconds. Run your knife around the edge of the bowl and blitz again. Add the grated sweet potato, honey and caraway seeds, before blitzing again until the mixture has come together and forms a damp dough.

3 Tip the contents of the food processor on to a floured surface and, with light fingers, bring the dough together into a rough ball shape. Please don't push or pressurize this dough too much – scones really are precocious, tricky creatures that don't react well to a heavy-handed approach. Gently roll out a smallish, thickish circle – again without applying too much pressure – roughly 20cm in diameter by 3cm deep.

4 Cut out ten circles and place them on the prepared baking sheet. Dust the tops of each one with a pinch of flour before placing in the oven for **15 minutes** until risen and golden.

TRUST ME TIPS

• Use a proper cutter where possible to achieve the best 'yawn' as it has a sharper, thinner edge than a glass or little bowl. Don't chisel into the mixture, but rather slice into it, otherwise the scones rise willy-wonky.

• Don't be alarmed that the mixture that comes out of the food processor appears slightly damp. This is normal, but if you feel it's a little *too* wet, simply knead in a little extra flour.

GINGER STICKY TOFFEE PUDDING

THIS CAKE HAS LIVED ABROAD for twenty-four years and has changed his habits quite a bit: he no longer reads the same paper, nor has the same breakfast (although he's still very partial to sharp marmalade). What hasn't changed is that nothing in the world beats a pint of beer pulled from the tap or sticky toffee pudding.

SERVES 9

200g stoned dates, chopped
100g pecans
150g scrubbed, topped, tailed and finely grated **parsnip**
150g topped, tailed, peeled and finely grated courgette
50g peeled and finely grated raw ginger
2 medium free-range eggs
2 tbsp clear honey
2 tbsp black treacle
200g rice flour
2 tsp baking powder
1 tsp bicarbonate of soda
¼ tsp salt
1 tbsp ground ginger

FOR THE SAUCE

120g unsalted butter
2 tsp black treacle
4 tbsp clear honey
¼ tsp salt
150ml black tea, such as English Breakfast (made with boiling water and a tea bag)
1 tsp ground ginger

YOU WILL NEED

a 22cm-square x 5cm-deep brownie tin
a food processor

1 Preheat the oven to 180°C/350°F/gas mark 4. Line the base of the tin with baking parchment. Using a little butter on your fingers, or some vegetable oil on a brush, lightly grease the parchment and the sides of the tin.

2 Start off by soaking the dates in a small bowl of boiling water (enough just to cover them). Cover quickly with cling film and set aside to steam and soak quietly.

3 Tip the pecans into the bowl of the food processor. Blitz to as close to powder as possible. Scrape down the bottom and sides of the bowl and blitz again. Add the grated parsnip, courgette and ginger to the food processor and blend to incorporate them with the pecans.

4 Drain the dates of their water. Next add the soaked dates, eggs, honey and treacle to the bowl of the food processor and whizz to combine. Finally, add the flour, baking powder, bicarbonate of soda, salt and ground ginger. Whizz one last time.

5 Tip the mixture into the prepared tin and place it in the middle of the oven for **1 hour**, placing a sheet of foil over the top of the cake after 30 minutes to prevent it from catching.

6 Remove the cake from the oven and cool it in the tin whilst you make the sticky toffee sauce.

7 To make the sticky toffee sauce, put all the ingredients into a small saucepan and bring to the boil. With the help of a timer (this is an exact science, I'm afraid), boil hard for 4 minutes. Take the sauce off the heat and give it a stir with your whisk.

8 You can either drench the cake in syrup inside the tin before cutting it up and serving, or you can cut it and then pour the sauce over. It goes without saying that this is utterly amazing with a little vanilla or ginger ice cream.

TRUST ME TIPS

• Great news! Not only do you not have to peel the vegetables, but you benefit from the awesome goodness contained in their skin. Just think of all that goodness rocking and rolling around your system!

• Feel free to replace the pecans with walnuts, or mix in a few brazil nuts if you don't have enough pecans in the house.

• I'm sorry to say that a food processor is really important here, since not only do the nuts need to be powdered, but this recipe won't work unless the dates are blitzed as well.

• It's a good idea to make the sauce ahead of time, but remember to keep it in the saucepan it was made in so that you can reheat it easily just before serving. Do not bring it to the boil again, however, or you will thicken it too much.

COFFEE AND WALNUT COURAGE CAKE For Kit

SOME WEEKS LOOM UP like mountain chains ahead. This cake is here to 'kiss it better' and give you a gently nudge. Coffee is brave, and walnuts are so reliable and sound that nothing in the world could ever push them into panic.

SERVES 12

200g white rice flour
120g walnuts
3 medium free-range
    eggs
160g light Muscovado
    sugar
250g scrubbed, topped,
    tailed and very
    finely grated **carrot**
2 tsp baking powder
¼ tsp salt
5 tbsp (125ml) coffee
    essence (such as
    Camp; see page
    180 for stockists)

FOR THE ICING

50g unsalted butter,
    cold and cubed
250g icing sugar, sieved
75g mascarpone
3 tsp coffee essence

FOR THE TOP

70g whole walnuts

YOU WILL NEED

two 18cm-diameter x
    5cm-deep loose-
    bottomed tins
a food processor

1 Preheat the oven to 180°C/350°F/gas mark 4. Line the bases of the tins with baking parchment. Lightly brush the parchment and the sides of the tins with a little vegetable oil.

2 Place the flour and walnuts in the bowl of the food processor and blitz them together until they are well mixed. The walnuts will never quite turn to dust, but they will get really small and make the flour look a bit like wholemeal flour (flecked with bits of blitzed walnut). Don't be surprised that this stage takes at least 4 minutes.

3 In a large mixing bowl, beat together the eggs and sugar for 3 minutes with an electric whisk, until they are cappuccino coloured and tripled in volume.

4 Add the grated carrot and beat again until incorporated. Add the flour and ground-walnut mixture, as well as the baking powder and salt. Beat until combined. Finally, add the coffee essence and mix again until all the ingredients are well introduced and the mixture is evenly coloured.

5 Divide the mixture evenly into the prepared tins, and bake in the middle of the oven for **30 minutes** exactly. Remove from the oven and cool on a wire rack whilst you make the icing.

6 To make the icing, whisk the butter with an electric whisk until softened and fluffy. Add 100g of the icing sugar and whisk to a paste. Next, add the mascarpone and coffee essence, as well as the remaining icing sugar. Beat with a wooden spoon to combine.

7 Refrigerate the icing for 15 minutes before filling the middle and icing the top of the cold cake. Finish the cake off by planting the walnuts into the icing on the top of the cake.

Cake Diaries

HEARTACHE CHOCOLATE CAKE

Testing Number 1: 17 March

I'm hoping for torte rather than cake but at this stage who can tell what will happen. I didn't have any tears to provide for the mixture, which is a shame, especially when you think of how many I had to spare yesterday. Still, the day outside is gratifyingly glum so all is not lost. I feel that the tin should be round, possibly even a fluted tart tin; we'll have to see how together the cake is when cooled . . . Well, it's bitter (as heartache should be!). The texture is far too lumpy – I'm thinking about cooking the aubergine next time. Also the nuts need to be made 'meal'. It's not a total failure but it's not nice. The most important aspect is smoothness – I'm looking for velvet softness and intensity.

Testing Number 3: 17 March

Well, I've tacked into the wind and gone a completely different route: aubergine purée in the hope of furnishing this heartache with silk. I am seeking a deep breath, followed by an exhalation. Much like a sob, come to think of it.

Testing Number 4: 17 March

Wow. I was beginning to feel quite close to defeat there, but now feel much closer to cracking it, I'm relieved to say. I'm pleased with the fragile state of the texture, which is both reassuring as well as vulnerable. There is a slight heave but not a substantial one yet. It's hard to believe that I could meet a sadder cake. There is unexpected dignity there, and a dash of 'I will survive' too.

Testing Number 5: 19 March

Looks and smells fantastic! My only worry is that it might not be vulnerable enough – it seems fairly together and sorted. Maybe the answer is ten minutes less in the oven.

Testing Number 6: 2 April

I *love* the cracks on the surface of the cake – proper heartbroken stuff! I'm going to wait for an outside opinion as I can't decide if it's chocolatey enough yet.

Testing Number 7: 3 April

I'm deeply hopeful for this little friend! The mixture tastes fantastic in its raw state and I like the relatively liquid aspect of the mixture since it suggests puff to come. We'll see . . . Another fifteen minutes to wait. Whatever happens, I'm moving on to St Clement's Cupcakes after this – I'm getting a chocolate headache and am murderous for a sharp citrus slap . . . It needs to cool in the tin for twenty minutes . . . The taste is fantastic. Slightly raw and tender – just like a heart. I'm happy at last. Serves fourteen – or a couple of seriously upset little sausages. Boy, it's rich.

CHOCOLATE AND CHESTNUT ROULADE

Testing Number 1: 28 November

This is a new tack at the eleventh hour. Maybe it's worth beating up the egg yolks and sugar with the cocoa next time since it feels that they are enthusiastic enough to take on the slight cocoa low. Hopefully this will provide more air. Really quite a pleasing result! A bit of a diplomat perhaps. Nearly there.

Testing Number 2: 28 November
Great! Hurrah for roly-poly roulades!

CHOCOLATE FULL STOPS

Testing Number 1: 7 May
These just sort of appeared in my mind because I wanted lots of little somethings to take to Talia's engagement drinks tomorrow night. Adorable, tiddly little creatures. I'm just looking for a light-hearted chocolate punch to finish the night and conclude. This one's bound to be a favourite in the making for Granny.

PARSNIP VANILLA FUDGE

Testing Number 1: 25 September
This is a fully experimental endeavour and drenched in science. I feel a bit demoralized today. Let's wait and see how this fudge behaves, and maybe just go for a bath if everything goes wrong.

Testing Number 2: 26 September
You will definitely need patience and the power of observation to tackle this recipe. Went and rolled up my sleeves in preparation for the 'megabeat' and found that I simply couldn't move the mixture at all – it was too heavy and had surreptitiously already turned into fudge! It's great, but too hard and too much like tablet.

Testing Number 3: 26 September
If the second version was like tablet, this version is like toffee.

Testing Number 4: 29 September
I have a sinking feeling that this fella might be complex. Oh dear. Enough today, something's not quite right. Maybe a swim will help.

Testing Number 7: 30 September
I've mopped the sweat off my brow. I'm there at long last.

COFFEE AND WALNUT COURAGE CAKE

Testing Number 1: 12 March
Should be named 'horror' as it gave me such a shock. A truly awful result. I'm going to freeze it as it's so vile it deserves to be isolated! Some quite frightening thoughts of 'Oh dear, what have I taken on?' came and went all day. What a mess. I've had to draw a line under this little disaster and move on to a more generous and feminine recipe. Luckily, she did appear to calm my fears and capture the imagination.

Testing Number 3: 2 April
It's a totally different creature altogether this time round, although it was still very liquid and insecure when it went into the tin. I'm not that optimistic but refuse to be defeated just yet!

Testing Number 4: 2 April
This is 100 per cent failure. It looks like a bread brick and tastes terribly bitter. It's really not nice. Oh dear, how discouraging. I'm so sorry. I feel like I've taken two steps back. I'm going to stop for the day.

Testing Number 5: 9 November
I haven't been able to face this old friend for a few months! Now that I have found some courage, I've taken him on again. This time I'm using Camp coffee essence and have completely re-jigged the texture . . . Wowee. We finally got there in the end. It was all worth it and I'm glad I waited and gave it another go.

STOCKISTS

Equipment

• My favourite **fine graters** are by Cuisipro and can be found online at www.mulberryhall.co.uk, or at most department stores.

• My **Magimix** was a 'hand-me-down' from my mother and has been with me for a long time, but is now on its last legs and being held together with sticky tape. All department stores and cookery shops will stock them and they are an invaluable piece of kitchen equipment.

• **Masterclass tins,** available from Kitchen Craft, are good for 20cm-square brownie tins, 18cm-diameter loose-bottomed tins and loaf tins, amongst others.
www.kitchencraft.co.uk
0121 604 6000

• **Prestige tins** are great for muffin trays, amongst others.
www.prestige.co.uk
0151 482 8282

• **Silverwood tins** are great for square tins, such as the ones needed for August Wedding Cake. They also produce a multi-size cake pan – an ingenious idea!
www.alansilverwood.co.uk
0121 454 3571

• My reliable (and inexpensive) **electric whisk** is from Kenwood, and is called: White Hand Mixer.
www.kenwoodworld.com
0239 239 2333

• For accuracy, I like to use digital **kitchen scales**. It is best to go for a set that can take 3kg and above. Salter has an excellent range, which is reliable and affordable.
www.salterkitchenscales.co.uk

• A good **rubber spatula** is a must-have. With a silicone head that is heatproof to 425°F, I recommend Le Creuset's medium spatulas. Plus, they come in lots of great colours.
www.lecreuset.co.uk
0800 373 792

• I use a clean paintbrush from a hardware store as a **pastry brush**. Otherwise, try Lakeland for a traditional wooden-handled one with good thick, natural bristles.
www.lakeland.co.uk
01539 488 100

• There's nothing like Mason Cash **mixing bowls** for size (they go up to 35cm diameter), quality and old-school style.
www.rayware.co.uk
0151 486 1888

Ingredients

• For the best organic **fruit and vegetables** delivered to your door, try Abel & Cole. www.abelandcole.co.uk 0845 262 6364

• Doves Farm makes my favourite cake ingredient, after vegetables: **white rice flour**. They also make an excellent **white spelt flour** (for the scones in the book). www.dovesfarm.co.uk 01488 684 880

• I find Cotswold Legbar or Burford Browns to be the best **free-range eggs** on the market. These eggs are available from most well-stocked supermarkets and are supplied by Clarence Court. www.clarencecourt.co.uk 01579 345 718

• My preferred brand for **peppermint extract, almond extract, lemon extract, orange blossom water** and **rose water** is Star Kay White, which is readily available in well-stocked supermarkets. www.starkaywhite.com

• Nielsen-Massey Madagascan Bourbon **vanilla extract** is the best for flavour and is available from most supermarkets, or online at Lakeland. www.lakeland.co.uk 01539 488 100

• I buy Camp **coffee essence** from my local supermarket, but if you can't find it there, then look for it online at www.temptingfoods.com

• The best **sweet chestnut purée** on the market is made by Clement Faugier and is called Crème de Marrons de l'Ardèche. Although this is a French product, I have found it at my local big supermarket. Failing this, you can buy it online at www.clementfaugier.fr.

• Sugarflair **food colouring paste** is available in lots of different colours. Remember, only the tiniest amount is needed . . . www.craftcompany.co.uk 01926 888 507

• For the Mulled White Wine Jellies, edible **gold leaf** is available from Squires Kitchen. www.squires-shop.com 0845 225 5671

• **Gelatine leaves** are not as common as the granulated form, but Costa Fine Leaf Gelatine (quick dissolving) can be found in most well-stocked supermarkets. Otherwise, it can be bought online at www.britstore.co.uk.

• For excellent quality **cooking chocolate** and **cocoa powder**, you'll find Green & Black's hard to beat.
www.greenandblacksdirect.com
020 7633 5900

• For an excellent alternative to cow's butter, I recommend St Helen's Farm **goat's butter**. This is now available at most well-stocked supermarkets, or you can visit www.sthelensfarm.co.uk.

Cake cases and decorations

If you love decorating cakes and cupcakes with colourful and imaginative **cases and sprinkles**, here are a few places to get some inspiration:

www.cottagecooks.co.uk
www.cupcakewrappers.co.uk
www.squires-shop.com
www.cakescookiesandcrafts.co.uk
www.lindyscakes.co.uk
www.design-a-cake.co.uk

Cakes 4 Fun
100 Lower Richmond Road
London SW15 1LN
020 8785 903
www.cakes4fun.co.uk

Jane Asher Party Cakes and Sugarcraft
22–24 Cale Street
London SW3 3QU
020 75846177
www.jane-asher.co.uk

La Cuisinière,
81–83 Northcote Road
London
SW11 6PJ
020 7223 4487
www.la-cuisiniere.co.uk

• **Cake boards** for August Wedding Cake can be found at specialist cake shops, such as the ones listed above.

NUTRITIONAL INFORMATION

CAKES (PER SERVING)	CALORIES (kcal)	SATURATED FAT (g)
Almond Honey Cake with Apricots and Vanilla	255	12.5
American Vanilla Cupcakes	180	1.1
August Wedding Cake	312	12.9
Autumn Apple and Cider Cake	227	8.5
Banana and Toffee Sticky Cake	340	18.5
Beach and Blanket Fruit Cake	288	10.8
Beetroot Chocolate Fudge	162	4.4
Birthday Cake	419	15.2
Cappuccino Cupcakes	282	10.8
Caramel Swiss Roll with Passionfuit Cream	335	14.2
Carrot Cake	350	14.0
Cherry and Almond Cake	293	3.5
Chocolate and Cherry Brandy Cupcakes	225	7.0
Chocolate and Chestnut Roulade	285	14.2
Chocolate and Peanut Butter Cupcakes	225	9.3
Chocolate and Salted Caramel Squillionaire	372	18.7
Chocolate Chocolate Chip Cupcakes	310	14.7
Chocolate Full Stops	52	1.6
Christmas Cupcakes	279	7.8
Cinnamon Banana Bread	204	5.9
Coconut Cake with Coconut Icing	313	12.5
Coconut, Lime and Blueberry Slice	262	7.0
Coffee and Walnut Courage Cake	418	20.0

	CALORIES (kcal)	SATURATED FAT (g)
Courgette and Camomile Cupcakes	183	3.4
Forbidden Chocolate Brownies	260	13.0
Ginger Millies	50	1.4
Ginger Sticky Toffee Pudding	440	20.0
Heartache Chocolate Cake	216	10.0
Honey and Sunflower Ginger Scones	142	4.5
Lavender Cupcakes	204	6.6
Lemon and Lavender Drizzle Cake	183	5.6
Lemon Drops	53	1.4
Lemon, Sunflower Seed and Blueberry Muffins	254	11.4
Light Chocolate Cake	273	10.6
Mint Choc Chip Cupcakes	303	13.4
Miss Marple Seed Cake	182	4.5
Orange and Cardamom Steamed Sponge	221	4.5
Orange and Rosemary Drizzle Cake	165	6.7
Orange and Saffron Sand Cake	301	7.6
Orange Blossoms	50	1.4
Orange Squash Cupcakes	266	16.1
Parmesan and Paprika Scones	136	2.5
Parsnip Vanilla Fudge	124	2.2
Peach and Poppy Seed Muffins	176	6.0
Pear and Pecan Calvados Cake	258	10.2
Pecorino and Chive Scones with Walnuts	141	4.6
Pistachio Chocolate Cake	308	15.8
Pistachio Pops	53	1.5

	CALORIES (kcal)	SATURATED FAT (g)
Plum Pudding	273	6.3
Port Mary Scones	165	5.0
Raspberry and Elderflower Cupcakes	221	6.6
Red Velvet Cake	407	19.1
Rosewater Fairy Cakes	206	5.7
St Clement's Cupcakes	216	3.8
Steamed Golden Syrup Sponge Pudding	224	5.3
Stem Ginger Syrup Cake	219	6.0
Strawberries and Cream Cupcakes	304	10.9
Sunken Apricot and Almond Cake	269	12.8
Sweet Potato and Caraway Scones	138	3.8
Syrup Scones	174	3.8
Treacle Steamed Sponge	287	10.3
Vanilla Cream and Raspberry Swiss Roll	371	12.0
Victoria Sponge	295	4.1
White Chocolate, Cinnamon and Raspberry Blondie	265	13.3
White Rabbits	51	1.6

JAMS (PER 30ML)

	CALORIES (kcal)	SATURATED FAT (g)
Blackberry Jam	74	trace
Bonfire Blackcurrant Jam	75	trace
Seedless Raspberry jam	160	0.2
Sharpie Strawberry Jam	80	trace
Sour Cherry Jam	113	0.2

INDEX

Page numbers in **bold** denotes an illustration

ACKNOWLEDGEMENTS

THE SPIRIT OF *Red Velvet & Chocolate Heartache* was nurtured by those who, with energy and talent, poured themselves into the making of this book. It is with a mountain of gratitude that I thank Becky Jones (godmother of *Red Velvet*), 'Fab Tab' Hawkins, Lucy Gowans, Joss Herd, Annie Rigg, Laura Fyfe, Biz Barne, Kate James, Jean Cazals, Phil Lord, Tim Jenner, Camilla Baynham and Rachel Walters. It takes a special sort of person to go to the end of what they have set out to do. Thank you for going there over and over again.

Transworld have been exceptional in giving me the freedom to get on with writing this book in my own way, and in showing the enthusiasm, trust and support that they have done over the last eighteen months.

And for the beautiful pictures, thank you to all the busy ballerinas . . . Florence, June, Iris (brought by lovely Aunty Alice), Chloe, Ruby, Laurie and Clara. Not forgetting Ben the Bear, who sits on a chair.

I am (as ever) so thankful for the encouragement and hard work of Rosemary Scoular, Chris Cope and Wendy Millyard at United Agents.

I would like to thank with glittering gratefulness my sister Georgina who means the world to me, and is without doubt the most perfect Mince Pie ever dreamed up.

During the testing phase of this book, I made a messy Cake Camp at my grandparents' house! To my dear friend Pooh (Granny Anne), I want to say a very *big* thank you. Not only have you taught me about the things in life that *really* matter (like blue sky and chocolate), but you also believed in my cakes every day for six months. Your patience and kindness heaved me through the grey days, and helped me skip through the yellow ones.

I'm sending a wink and a nod to a small number of special people: Camilla Gruzman, Will Fraser, Polly and Tom Allen, Bellsie Arbuthnott, Talia Williams, Henny Acloque, Jo McGrath, Sarah Tildesley, Mike Sinclair, and the immortal Valentina Morales.

Thank you to my adored aunt and uncle, Sarah and Johnny Van Haeften, for their immense kindness in letting us shoot in both their house and doll's house.

Finally, thank you, Doug Young, for your vision and courage in commissioning this book. By the way, you *are* Treacle Steamed Sponge . . . x